MEMOIR

OF THE LIFE OF

HENRY-FRANCIS D'AGUESSEAU,

CHANCELLOR OF FRANCE;

AND OF HIS

ORDONNANCES FOR CONSOLIDATING AND AMENDING

CERTAIN PORTIONS OF

THE FRENCH LAW:

AND

AN HISTORICAL AND LITERARY ACCOUNT

OF

THE ROMAN AND CANON LAW.

FOURTH EDITION.

BY

CHARLES BUTLER, ESQ.

BARRISTER AT LAW.

THE LAWBOOK EXCHANGE, LTD.

Clark, New Jersey

2008

ISBN-13: 978-1-58477-746-5
ISBN-10: 1-58477-746-X

The quality of this reprint is equivalent to the quality of the original work.

THE LAWBOOK EXCHANGE, LTD.
33 Terminal Avenue
Clark, New Jersey 07066-1321

Please see our website for a selection of our other publications and fine facsimile reprints of classic works of legal history:
www.lawbookexchange.com

Library of Congress Cataloging-in-Publication Data

Butler, Charles, 1750-1832.
Memoir of the life of Henry-Francis D'Aguessau, Chancellor of France : and of the ordonnances for consolidating and amending certain portions of the French law : and an historical and literary account of the Roman and Canon law / by Charles Butler.
p. cm.
Previously published: 4th ed. London, J. Murray, 1830.
Includes bibliographical references.
ISBN-13: 978-1-58477-746-5 (alk. paper)
ISBN-10: 1-58477-746-X (alk. paper)
1. Aguesseau, H. Fr. d' (Henri François), 1668-1751. 2. Lawyers--France--Biography. 3. Statesmen--France--Biography. 4. Roman law--History. 5. Canon law--History. I. Aguesseau, H. Fr. d' (Henri François), 1668-1751. II. Title.
KJV251.5.A48B88 2005
340.092--dc22
[B]

2006017685

Printed in the United States of America on acid-free paper

MEMOIR

OF THE LIFE OF

HENRY-FRANCIS D'AGUESSEAU,

CHANCELLOR OF FRANCE;

AND OF HIS

ORDONNANCES FOR CONSOLIDATING AND AMENDING

CERTAIN PORTIONS OF

THE FRENCH LAW:

AND

AN HISTORICAL AND LITERARY ACCOUNT

OF

THE ROMAN AND CANON LAW.

FOURTH EDITION.

BY

CHARLES BUTLER, ESQ.

BARRISTER AT LAW.

LONDON:

JOHN MURRAY, ALBEMARLE-STREET;

AND

J. & W.T. CLARKE, PORTUGAL-STREET, LINCOLN'S-INN.

M.DCCC.XXX.

Quare quis tandem me reprehendat, aut quis mihi jure succenseat, si, quantum cæteris ad suas res obeundas, quantum ad festos dies ludorum celebrandos, quantum ad alias voluptates, et ad ipsam requiem animi et corporis conceditur temporis: quantum alii, tribuunt tempestivis conviviis: quantum denique aleæ, quantum pilæ; tantum mihi egomet ad hæc studia recolenda sumsero?

CICERO pro Archiâ Poetâ.

Printed by James & Luke G. Hansard & Sons,
near Lincoln's-Inn Fields, London.

CONTENTS.

CHAPTER VII.

CHAPTER VIII.

MEMOIR

OF THE LIFE OF

HENRY-FRANCIS D'AGUESSEAU,

CHANCELLOR OF FRANCE.

CHAPTER THE FIRST.

INTRODUCTION.

THERE is no condition, in which transcendent excellence in the discharge of its duties is more beneficial, either to the State, or to the individuals who compose it, than that of a magistrate, who presides in one of its supreme tribunals, and whose counsels considerably influence its civil legislation.

Such was Henry-Francis D'Aguesseau, Chancellor of France. Profoundly skilled in its constitution and laws, intimately versed in literature and science, a sincere lover of his country, religious, upright, indefatigable, patient and considerate, he filled, during thirty-four years, the highest of its magisterial dignities. In his discharge of it, his wisdom was never called in question, his integrity never suspected. He was the author of many legislative provisions, which are universally esteemed. He left behind him many works, replete with erudition, and abounding with lessons of the purest and most useful morality. There is no country in which they may not be read, particularly by persons engaged in the study or practice of jurisprudence, with the greatest advantage and pleasure.

In perusing the ensuing biographical account of the Chancellor D'Aguessau, our readers should bear in mind the following circumstances.

According to the *antient régime of France*, the kingdom was divided into the *Pays du droit écrit* and the *Pays coutumier*. The provinces of Guyenne, Provence, Dauphiné, and, speaking generally, all the territories within the jurisdictions of the Parliaments of Toulouse, Aix, Pau, and Bourdeaux, and some within the jurisdiction of the Parliament of Paris, as the Lyonese, the Forez, the Beaujolois, and a great part of Auvergne, were included in the former; the rest of France was included on the latter. The *Pays du droit écrit* was governed by the Roman law—the territories of the *Pays coutumier*, by its several local laws and customs. From this, the two divisions of France took their distinctive appellations. But in many cases particular customs had been admitted into the former, and some rules of Roman jurisprudence had been admitted into the latter.

In each of these divisions, there was a *written* and *unwritten* law, corresponding, in their nature, with the laws designated by these terms in English jurisprudence. For an obvious reason, in the *Pays du droit écrit*, the Roman law was part of its written, in the *Pays du droit coutumier*, it was part of its unwritten law.

France had twelve Parliaments,—those of Paris, Toulouse, Grénoble, Bourdeaux, Dijon, Rouen, Aix, Rennes, Pau, Metz, Douai, and Besançon. Of these, the Parliament of Paris was the most antient, and by far the most considerable in its rights and powers: to this Parliament we confine what is said in the following lines.

The Parliament consisted of the king, the chancellor, a first president, nine other presidents, six ecclesiastical peers, three of whom were dukes, three counts, the lay peers, the honorary counsellors, the *maîtres des requêtes*, the clerical and lay counsellors, the three *avocats généraux*, the *procureur général*, some substitutes, and a multitude of officers.

The archbishop of Paris, and, in his absence, his coadjutor, was entitled to a seat in the parliament. Whether the king could in strictness be said to be a member, or a portion of the parliament, was disputed. He held his *Lit de Justice* in it, and, on some great occasions, as to enforce the registration of his edicts, summoned the members of the Parliament to attend him there.

It was on extraordinary occasions only that the chancellor was present at the assemblies of the Parliament.

It should also be observed, that between the Parliament of England, and those of France, there was scarcely any analogy: the Parliament of England is divided into two houses, that of the lords, and that of the commons; these, with the king, constitute the legislature of the nation; but, except for trials of peers, impeachments, and cases brought before the House of Lords by appeal, the Parliament of England exercises no judicial power. The Parliaments of France had no legislative authority; it was a high court of justice, for the last resort; a court for cases respecting the royal revenue, and other concerns of the state, or particular magnitude.*

* See, in Mr. Butler's REMINISCENCES, Vol. I. Art. III. Sect. His Remarks—1st, On the Heirship and Venality of Judicial Offices in France.—2d, On the Presents and Personal Solicitations to Foreign Judges.—3d, On the Limits of the Right of Courts of Judicature to interpret Laws.—4th, On the Separation of Courts of Law and Equity, peculiar to English Jurisprudence.—5th, On the Reductions and Reforms of the French Customary and Statute Law, and on the Code Napoleon.—6th, On the Order of Avocats in France, and its Extinction at the French Revolution.—7th, And On the English Law of Property.

In the following pages, we have availed ourselves of other parts of the same Work.

CHAPTER THE SECOND.

Henry D'Aguesseau, Father of the Chancellor.

ANTHONY D'AGUESSEAU, the grandfather of the chancellor, was successively *maître des requêtes*, president of the great council, counsellor of state, intendant of Picardy, and first president of the Parliament of Bourdeaux. "His reputation," says M. Thomas, in his *Eloge de D'Aguesseau*, "has reached "our times; his praise is consecrated in the "history of Saintonge."

Henry D'Aguesseau, the father of the chancellor, was counsellor in the Parliament of Metz, successively president of its council, *maître des requêtes*, intendant of the provinces of Limousin, Guienne, and Languedoc, and finally raised to the dignity of counsellor of state. All these offices were filled by him with distinguished honour and wisdom. The province of Languedoc offered him a large increase of the emoluments of his office;

he refused it. On a rumour of his death, they voted a public funeral, and a monument at the expense of the provinces.

In an interesting Memoir, entitled, "*Discours sur la Vie et la Mort de M. D'Aguesseau, Conseiller d'Etat,*" his son, the subject of the present biography, has consigned, in a very pleasing manner, an ample account of his father's public and private virtues, to posterity.

Of the offices we have mentioned, that of intendant was probably the most important. The person, on whom such an office was conferred, had the general superintendence of all the civil concerns of the crown within the province committed to his care; particularly the repartition of the taxes among the members of the department on which they were assessed. Here, he had to arrange the conflicting claims of the crown and the proprietors, and those of the latter among themselves. The consequence was, that the intendant was generally viewed with feelings of dislike; but the conduct of Henry D'Aguesseau was so wise, just, and conciliating, that his arrival in any part of the province, in which he was to execute his office, always gave pleasure.

He took an active part, and was eminently useful in the completion of the celebrated canal of Languedoc. It begins near the Bay of Languedoc, and enters the Garonne at about a quarter of a league below Toulouse. Thus it joined the Mediterranean to the Atlantic. Its breadth, including the towing-paths, is one hundred and forty-four feet; its depth, six feet; its length, sixty-four French leagues, or about one hundred and eighty English miles. Much of the country, through which it flows, is either sandy or mountainous. Fifteen years of labour, from 1666 to 1681, were employed, and about half a million sterling was expended upon it. M. Riquet planned and conducted this magnificent enterprise. He had no mathematical knowledge: all that he knew of mechanics, he had taught himself; his only instrument was an indifferent iron compass. The chancellor D'Aguesseau informs us, that he often heard him mention this circumstance. By this canal, the artillery, by which Louis XIV. bombarded Genoa, was carried. The chancellor relates, with evident pleasure, that soon after the completion of the canal, his father, accompanied by him, made two journies along the canal, from the beginning to the end of its course.

In the eye of an Englishman, whether Catholic or Protestant, the conduct of the intendant D'Aguesseau, on the Revocation of the Edict of Nantes, will place him in an amiable and respectable point of view. He protested against the measure while it was in agitation, predicted its disastrous results, and, to avoid the view of them, resigned his intendancy. In the Memoir of his father's life, the chancellor thus expresses his father's sentiments and his own, on the conduct which the French Government ought to have pursued towards their Protestant subjects:—

" The maxims of my father, on the conver-
" sion of the Huguenots, were very simple,
" and quite conformable to the true spirit of
" the church; that we should preach to Pro-
" testants, instruct, and exhort them; that we
" should detach their chiefs and leaders from
" them; that we should call in aid privations,
" not civil penalties, to induce them, prejudiced

"as they are, to make salutary reflections; "that we should restrain and lessen, as far "as justice allows, their free liberty in the "exercise of their religion; that we should "favour the new converts, and restore to "them with usury the advantages of which, "but only for their good, they had been "deprived; in fine, that we should consider "the Protestant religion as a fortified city, "which it is not desirable to take by as-"sault; but that, if the expression may be "used, we should seize every day some por-"tion of its territory, till it should be reduced "so much, that the city must fall of itself." We acknowledge that there is much in this system, that religion, morality, and sound policy must disapprove; but, in the time of D'Aguesseau, it was highly honourable to advance thus far in the doctrine of toleration. *The Dialogues of Galileo* do him infinite honour, though the discoveries announced by them were afterwards wonderfully extended by the *Principia of Sir Isaac Newton*: the niggard liberality of D'Aguesseau should be allowed a just measure of praise, though it bears no proportion to the noble spirit of enlarged wisdom and policy shewn, in 1829, by the British Government to its Catholic subjects;—and which, we most earnestly pray and hope will soon be shewn to the Jews.

The chancellor then proceeds to recount, at some length, his father's other estimable and amiable qualities. We are sure our readers will peruse with pleasure the following short extract from it: "The rule of my "father and mother," says the chancellor, "for the regular exercise of charity, was, "to set apart for it a tenth of their income, "and at the end of the year, to divide their "savings into as many portions as they had "children, and one portion more; so that "if they had four children, and their "savings amounted to ten thousand livres, "they appropriated eight thousand to their "children, and gave the remaining two "thousand livres to the poor; treating them "as their children in Jesus Christ, by a holy "and glorious adoption. But public and "private calamities generally raised the por-"tion of the poor to a much larger sum than "they would have been entitled to receive "upon this calculation. We have seen, by

" the accounts of my father, that, in some " years, his alms exceeded twenty-two thou- " sand livres: one-third of the whole amount " of his income."

Henry D'Aguesseau died in 1715, having lived to behold his son filling some of the highest dignities of the magistrature of France with unblemished reputation, and the chancellorship and seals almost within his reach. He certainly was called to them by the universal wish of the bar, the bench, and all the virtuous and honourable part of the nation.

M. Thomas, in the second note to his *Eloge of the Chancellor*, says, that his father " possessed all the virtues, which great places " presuppose, but do not always confer. He " was just, disinterested, beneficent, a friend " of the people, a statesman, and an ex- " cellent father of a family. To all these " titles to our esteem he added one, which was " in his time common to all magistrates,—he " was learned." But nothing has recommended him to posterity so much as the excellent education which he gave to his son. It is gratefully mentioned by him, and dwelt upon with pleasure by all his biographers.

The Duke de St. Simon, niggard as he is of praise, bestows it with profusion on Henry D'Aguesseau: it is impossible to place any person in a more amiable or respectable light.

CHAPTER THE THIRD.

Birth and Education of the Chancellor D'Aguesseau.

HENRY-FRANCIS D'AGUESSEAU, was born at Limoges on the 16th of November 1668. His father has been mentioned; his mother was Clairelle Picart de Perigny, of a noble family. The father of the future chancellor was almost his only preceptor: all the biographers of the chancellor agree in their account of the excellent education, which he received from his father; of his unremitted diligence in prosecuting his studies, and the early indication given by him of a love of virtue. They inform us, that his father always made him his companion in the numerous journies, which the duties of his intendancies made necessary; that, both when he was stationary, and when he was travelling, his father always took care that he should be surrounded by men eminent for virtue and learning; and that the conversation should turn on useful topics. This excited in his son the highest degree of literary ardour. He soon discovered a virtuous heart, a mild and beneficent disposition, a great elevation of soul, great quickness of apprehension, great fertility of imagination, great soundness of judgment, and surprising mental activity. With these endowments, and his father's excellent cultivation of them, the extent and depth of his attainments will not surprise our readers. With the principles of his own language he was thoroughly acquainted; he was master of the Latin, Greek, Hebrew, Italian, Spanish, Portuguese, and English languages. So easily did he obtain the knowledge of them, that he always spoke of the acquisition of a new language as an amusement. Our readers will recollect the equally easy, but far more extensive acquisition of languages by our late distinguished countryman, Sir William Jones. The perusal of the antient poets was, to use his own words, "a passion of his youth." The company of Boileau and Raçine was his greatest delight, and almost his only recreation. The Greek and Roman authors were familiar to him; with the rules of logic and the artifices of dialectic, with the philosophy of Aristotle and Descartes, and with geometry and algebra, he was fully acquainted. He was intimately versed in every branch of sacred and ecclesiastical history and literature.

In an early period of life, he engaged in the study of the law; not with a view of practising at the bar, but to qualify himself to act as a magistrate, or, as we should express it, as a judge. A comparative account of the differences in the law and judicial institutions of France and England, would be an interesting and useful work; we hope to receive it from the pen of some English or Scottish jurist.

Speaking generally, in England, the judges of the royal courts are chosen from the barristers: all England would stand aghast at a different appointment. In France, no avocat or barrister was raised to the seat of a judge in a royal court. The wisdom of this arrangement is maintained by many respectable writers on the continent. To us, and, as we believe, to every Englishman, it must appear preposterous in the extreme. Still, we are not to suppose that the French judges were unlearned, because they were not taken from the bar. They always went regularly through previous courses of civil and canon law, and studied systematically the written and unwritten laws of their country. On these, they afterwards underwent a solemn and serious examination; if they were found deficient, they were either remanded for a further examination, or were absolutely rejected. The first volume of the quarto edition of the works of the Chancellor D'Aguesseau contains a "Discourse" addressed by him to his son "on the Study of the Laws." It shews the extensive reading and just views of the chancellor; but so little of this Discourse is applicable to the study of the law of England, that, although we are thoroughly sensible of its value, we shall make no further mention of it in this place.

The close of the fifteenth century is described by French writers as the golden age of the French magistracy. It is every where said, that the knowledge which the members of it possessed of the law, was at once extensive and profound, and that they were equally conversant in its theory and its practice; that they respected their profession, and were aware of the importance of a proper discharge of their duties; and that, while their undeviating attention and gravity convinced the lowest class of subjects that justice would be fully and impartially administered to them, they equally intimated to persons in the highest classes of society, that, in the scales of justice, rank was of no account.

At six o'clock in the morning, both winter and summer, the magistrates took their seats in court. At ten o'clock, the beadle entered the court, and announced the hour; they then went to dine. After dinner, they returned to their seats; at six o'clock, the business of the courts was closed; the rest of the day was devoted to their families: literary pursuits were their only relaxation. "To "feel," says the *Abbé Gédoyn*, in one of his entertaining memoirs, "that magistrates "were, in those days, more addicted than "they are in our times, to professional and "literary studies, it is sufficient to compare

" the state of Paris at that time with its pre-
" sent state. At the time we speak of, the
" police of Paris was very bad; the city
" was ill built, and had not half either of
" the houses or the inhabitants which it
" now contains. The streets were ill laid
" out, excessively dirty, never lighted, and
" therefore, after dusk, unsafe. The only
" public spectacles were vulgar farces, after
" which the populace ran with avidity, but
" which all decent persons avoided. Their
" meals were frugal; there was nothing in
" them to attract company; the fortunes of
" individuals were small, and parsimony was
" the only means of increasing them. A
" coach of any kind was hardly seen; per-
" sons of high rank walked on foot, in ga-
" loches or small boots, which, when they
" paid a visit of ceremony, they left in the
" antichamber, and resumed when they
" quitted it. The magistrates rode on mules
" when they went to courts of justice, or
" returned from them. It followed, that
" when a magistrate, after the sittings of
" the court, returned to his family, he had
" little temptation to stir again from home.

"His library was necessarily his sole re-
"source; his books his only company. Speak-
"ing generally, he had studied hard at col-
"lege, and had acquired there a taste for
"literature, which never forsook him. To
"this austere and retired life, we owe the
"Chancellor de L'Hopital, the President de
"Thou, Pasquier, Loisel, the Pithous, and
"many other ornaments of the magistracy.
"These days are passed; and they are passed
"because the dissipation of Paris is extreme.
"Is a young man of family now destined
"for the law? Before he attains his six-
"teenth year, a charge is obtained for him,
"and he sports a chariot. With such faci-
"lities of going and coming, what a wish
"must there be to be in every place where
"pleasure calls! Consider only the time
"given, even by persons of decent habits of
"life, to music and the opera! What a sub-
"traction it is from that portion of time
"which the magistrates of old gave to pro-
"fessional study and literature."

Admitting the general truth of the repre-
sentations given by the *Abbe Gédoyn*, of the
different habits and manners of the antient

and modern French magistracy, it may be thought that, in justice to the latter, he should have remarked, that, if the magistracy of his own times had receded from the austerity of their predecessors, all the other classes of society in France had made an equal advance into dissipation; so that the difference between them was, in the very last years of the *ancien régime*, as great as ever.

With the magistracy of France in the last century, and their general habits, the writer of these pages was well acquainted. All were eminently decent, and a large proportion of them was edifying. Most were literary, or lovers of the arts. They collected men of learning or science round them. There were societies, amusements, and other scenes of gaiety, which a respectable portion of the other classes thought open to them, but from which the magistrates of France and their families thought their character excluded them. All the magistrates were loyal, but sincerely attached to the antient constitution of their country. They were very attentive to the duties of their profession: they lived in their families; their relaxations were always suited to their character. Such were the Lamoignons, the D'Aguesseaus, the Pothiers, the Montesquieus, the Mallesherbes, the des Brosseses, the Seguiers, the Joly-de-Fleurys. It may be truly said, that the world has not produced a more learned, enlightened, or honourable order of men than the French Magistracy.

CHAPTER THE FOURTH.

D'Aguesseau,—Avocat Général and Procureur Général.

D'Aguesseau opened his judicial career by filling the offices of *the King's Avocat Général at the Châtelet.* He held this office only during a few months; but the talents he displayed raised the greatest expectations of the splendour of his future success. The celebrated Denys Talon, then President à Mortier, directing his look to him, said,—"I should wish to finish, as that young man "begins."

A third charge of *Avocat Général at the Parliament of Paris* having been created, his father solicited Louis XIV. to appoint his son to it. The monarch, although another candidate of great merit and connections was strongly pressed on him, immediately granted the request. "I am," he said, "so well ac"quainted with the merit of the father, that

"I know he will not deceive me, even when "he gives testimony in favour of his son." This appointment took place in 1691: D'Aguesseau was then only twenty-two years and one half old.

D'Aguesseau found time to answer the immense demands on his attention, which this office produced. Yet he went to the bottom of every thing, and often discovered important laws, valuable documents, material facts, and powerful arguments, which had escaped the attention of the gentlemen at the bar, and the judges. In his speeches, erudition, order, clearness, strength of reasoning and eloquence were happily combined. Persons might have imagined that his discourses were the effect of long preparation; but, except in cases of extreme importance, he only committed to paper short heads of what he intended to say. He spent the vacations in the country, amidst his family.

There, in 1700, he was found, when Louis XIV., on the recommendation of Harlai, the first President, conferred on him the superior office of *Procureur Général*. The duties of it he discharged with an ability and integrity that made him an object of universal admiration. These were particularly discernible in his attention to the administration of the hospitals, the prisons, and the provisions for the country poor. Great were his exertions to alleviate the general misery occasioned by the famine, which desolated France in the years 1709 and 1710. This he had foreseen; and, to lessen the impending calamity, had prevailed on Government to purchase immense quantities of corn before a suspicion of the famine arose, and augmented its price. He was very attentive to the administration of the criminal law: it was observed, that fewer criminals suffered while he held the offices we have mentioned, than during any former period of the same duration. The management of the estates of the Crown was a subject more congenial to his feelings: he used to say, that he wished the King to be thought the best landlord in France; still that the King should have all his dues, and either regularly receive, or regularly remit them.

Though he paid great regard to religion, and was most punctual and regular in the discharge of its duties, this did not blind him to the independence of the Crown on the spiritual power in temporal concerns. While he was engaged in the official situations we have mentioned, two events took place, which called for all his vigilance in this respect. In the contest respecting the book of the celebrated Fénélon, Archbishop of Cambray, entitled, "*Maximes des Saints*," Louis XIV. had made himself a party to the cause, and solicited the bull of the condemnation of the Archbishop's work, with all the ardour and pertinacity of a partisan. When the bull was promulgated, he received it with delight; and, to make it a law of the State, required the Parliament to register it. This, the Parliament, more jealous than the monarch himself, of his and the nation's rights and liberties, refused to do. The monarch received a similar refusal, on the Pope's condemnation of "*The Moral Reflections of Father Quesnel*," by the bull *Unigenitus*. Ultimately, both bulls were registered; but an opinion favourable to the registration of the latter was not obtained from D'Aguesseau. He has left an account of the principal circumstances, which took place on this occasion; it is very interesting. It contains admirable portraits of the great antagonists, Bossuet and Fénélon; the whole is written with senatorial gravity; but, in some parts, a lurking smile on the writer's countenance is discoverable. The memoir shews how slowly the just opinions now held on the papal temporal power obtained the ascendant.

Notwithstanding the opposition of D'Aguesseau, the bull *Unigenitus* was registered: he then recommended the parties, whose signature of it was required, to sign it. For this, he was blamed by the opposers of the bull; they described it as a contradiction of his former principles. In his defence, he justly observed, that it was one thing to object to a law, while it is a subject of deliberation; another, to recommend submission to it, after it was passed into a law. There was no inconsistency in Fénélon's defending the "Maxims of the Saints," before they were formally condemned, and his afterwards subscribing to their condemnation.*

* For an account of the controversies on the two bulls, we beg leave to refer our readers to the writer's "Life of

No one was more just to the merit of others, or more ready to oblige them, than D'Aguesseau. Numerous memorials and consultations, which could not be required from him, were, while he held the office of procureur-général, prepared by him for others with great care and labour. It was always pleasing to him to bring forward, and give due praise to the talents and virtues of his brother magistrates. On the death of M. le Nain, his intimate friend, who had succeeded him in his charge of avocat général, D'Aguesseau pronounced his elogium from the bench with so much eloquence and pathos, that he was obliged to pause for some minutes to give a vent to the feelings of himself and his auditory.

D'Aguesseau long enjoyed the favour of Louis XIV., but experienced, in consequence of his opposition to the registration of the bull *Unigenitus*, a visible decrease of the monarch's favour. At length, his removal from his office of procureur-général was

Fenelon," and his " History of the Church of France " during the Reign of Louis XIV. and Louis XV. and " the Revolution."

expected; and even something worse was apprehended. Many writers relate, that on one occasion D'Aguesseau was summoned to Versailles by an angry message, and that his wife, when he took his leave of her, said to him, "Go! and, while you are before "the King, forget your wife, forget your "children; lose every thing, except your "honour."

It greatly adds to the glory of D'Aguesseau, that in the first moment of his appearing in public life, he displayed the full extent of his endowments; and that he had not, among either his contemporaries or his predecessors, any model upon which he could form himself.

Pulpit oratory attained its greatest elevation in the reign of Louis XIV. *Patru* and *Le Maitre*, by far the most eminent of the forensic orators, who preceded D'Aguesseau, possessed little merit. At the present time, their plaidoyers are illegible. To D'Aguesseau's style of judicial oratory, the English will greatly prefer that of Lord Hardwicke, Lord Mansfield, and Sir William Grant. This will surprise their French neighbours;

but, when two such nations as the French and English differ on a matter of taste, each should respect the opinion of the other, and a little distrust his own.

Those who wish to see the nature of D'Aguesseau's eloquence, in his capacity of Avocat-Général, should read his Plaidoyer in the cause of the *Sieur de la Pivardière.* It is remarkable that D'Aguesseau on this occasion condemned, in strong terms, the ordonnance, which withheld from criminals accused, the assistance of pleading counsel.

The offices of Avocat-Général and Procureur-Général required of D'Aguesseau that he should pronounce the discourses designated in France, by the name of *Mercuriales.* Certain Edicts of Charles VIII., Louis XII., and Henry III., directed that, in the assemblies customarily held on the Wednesdays (*dies Mercurii*) immediately following the feast of Saint Martin and Michaelmas-day, one of the king's law-officers should address to the audience, after the reading of the ordonnances, a discourse on the duties of their charge. From 1693 to 1715, both years included, D'Aguesseau, then Avocat-

Général or Procureur-Général, pronounced their discourses nineteen times. The subjects of them were, the independence, the love of his state, the due regard to public opinion, the greatness of soul, the dignity, the taste for simplicity, the blameless morals and manners, the literature and science, the attachment to the service of the public, the authority and submission to law, the spirit of justice, the right views of it, the self-respect, the profound professional learning, the fixed and persevering attention, the firmness, the proper employment of time, the impartiality, the regularity, and the love of his country, which a Judge ought to possess. On all these subjects, D'Aguesseau expresses himself with eloquence, chastened by good sense and taste. The great difficulty attending discourses of this kind is to avoid common-place, and to speak feelingly, but without apparent effort. This D'Aguesseau successfully accomplished. His *Mercuriales* were universally admired: pocket editions of them were published; they were considered to be the moral code of the magistracy of France.

CHAPTER THE FIFTH.

D'Aguesseau, as Chancellor of France.

IN all countries of Europe, the chancellor is the highest dignitary of the state, the guardian of the sovereign's conscience, and ordinarily the keeper of his seal; the visitor of the hospitals and colleges of the king's foundation, and the general superintendant of charitable foundations. Beyond these, the chancellors of England exercise, but sometimes in consequence of the introduction of trusts, a vast and extensive jurisdiction, partly as a court of common law, but principally as a court of equity. On the continent, the chancellors have no such exclusive court, but have universal superintendance over all that relates to the administration of justice in the kingdom, a controlling power to correct any abuses, which find their way into courts of judicature, to form new regulations for their proceedings, to determine questions of jurisdiction between them, to settle differences among the members of them, to appoint the higher offices of justice, and frame the royal ordonnances and edicts which in anywise relate to the legal polity of the kingdom, or the administration of justice. In most countries, the administration of common law and equity is committed to the same courts; in England the courts are separate. Lord Bacon (*De Augmentis Scientiarum, Sect. III. Chap.* 3. *Art.* 45.) has pronounced a decisive opinion in favour of their separation.

On the death of the Chancellor Voisin, in the beginning of February 1717, the Regent immediately determined to confer on D'Aguesseau the vacant dignity.

He sent an officer to D'Aguesseau to request his immediate attendance upon him. The messenger found D'Aguesseau at mass in the parish church of Frésnes, a village, in which his country-house was situate. On receiving the message, D'Aguesseau desired the messenger to inform the Regent that he would attend him, as soon as possible, after the mass should be finished. He then proceeded to the Regent at the *Palais Royal*, the residence of the Orleans family: the Regent addressed him by the title of chancellor, would not listen to the wish he expressed to decline the office, and coolly informed him, that he had appointed his particular friend M. Joly de Fleury procureur-général, in his stead. Never was an appointment of a chancellor more applauded. On the following day, D'Aguesseau took the customary oaths of office, before the infant king.

D'Aguesseau had then just reached his forty-eighth year.

From the time of his appointment to this high office, till his resignation of it, a period, as we have already observed, of thirty-four years, he dedicated himself entirely to the discharge of his important functions. That he possessed, in the highest degree, the knowledge of every branch of French jurisprudence, in the most extensive sense of the word; that he was intimately acquainted with the institutions and customs of the nation; that he had the soundest notions of civil polity; that his integrity and honour were above suspicion; that his application to business was unremitted; that his eloquence, both on great and ordinary occasions, was admirable; that he was always patient, and always easy of access; that he was loyal to his sovereign, and a true friend of the people,—is universally acknowledged.

The commencement of the regency was distinguished by the *Mississippi* project of the celebrated John Law, of Lauriston, in North Britain. In May 1716, a bank was established in favour of that adventure: it consisted of twelve hundred shares, each of 5,000 livres. In January 1718, the regent reimbursed the proprietors, and took the bank into the hands of the crown: it then received the name of "*The Royal Bank;*" it was placed under the direction of Law. It prospered; and instantaneously produced in France, particularly in the capital, a general taste for stock-jobbing and paper money speculation. Upon this, Law formed a scheme for establishing a great commercial company. All the privileges, possessions, and effects of the foreign trading companies were to be transferred to it; the revenue of the crown was to be vested in it; the royal bank was to be attached to it; the whole province of Louisiana was to be granted to it; the name of "The Company "of the West" was to be given to it; and Law was to govern it. The regent acquiesced in the plan, established the company, and conferred on it all that Law solicited. From the river Mississippi, on which the province of Louisiana lies, the project obtained the appellation of "*The Mississippi Scheme.*" By subsequent patents, the regent granted to the company the right of exclusive trade to China and every part of the East Indies; this gave it the name of "The Company of the Indies."

It was held out to the public, that these enormous possessions and enormous powers would enable the company to atchieve adventures in commerce, which would rapidly bring the whole wealth of the world into its hands, and entitle the shareholders to dividends far exceeding the greatest gains of the most successful adventurer in those or former times. The company actually announced a dividend of 200 per cent. The delusion became general, and rose to such a height, that in September 1721, the price of shares was more than sixty times the amount of that for which they had originally sold; and the bank lent money on the slightest security at two per cent. Things thus continued till the 21st of the following May. During this period, the public creditors were paid with notes of the bank of France, which they accepted as cash, and the former securities given them by the crown were withdrawn and cancelled. But, on that memorable day, a royal arrêt revealed the true nature of the bubble: the paper fabric was instantaneously blown away; and on the following morning, (the 22d of May), a man might have starved with paper for one hundred millions in his pocket.

The general result was, that an immense number of individuals were ruined, and the greater part reduced to the most abject poverty; but the State was a gainer. The national debt, when the scheme was first adopted, amounted to eighty millions of French livres; it was reduced, by the paper-operations, to fifty-seven millions: the twenty-three millions, which made the difference, were the gain of the State.

When the project was first proposed to the regent, a council of state was held upon it.

At this time, D'Aguessau was procureur-général; he opposed the measure. He predicted both its first success, and its ultimate disasters; and that each would equally be ruinous to the country, and an immense multitude of individuals. His arguments prevailed, and, for that time, the project was abandoned. The advocates of it persisted in recommending it to the regent, and finally brought him over to their views. In the meantime, D'Aguesseau had become chancellor; he persisted in his opposition: he was then, as the French term it, disgraced; that is, the seals were taken from him, and he was banished to his country residence at Frésnes. The seals were placed in the hands of *M. D'Argenson.* The general calamity produced by the failure of the Mississippi scheme, compelled the regent to recall D'Aguesseau from his banishment, and the seals were then restored to him. A memorable consultation then took place; it was debated in council, whether the state should pay the national creditors as far as its resources extended, or declare itself bankrupt, retaining the funds without making any distribution of them among the creditors. Most of the royal advisers inclined to the latter operation; but the chancellor contended strenuously for the former. He observed, that "what was dishonourable seldom proved expedient;" and finally brought over the council to his opinion.

But the favour of the chancellor at the corrupt court of the regent could not be long. He was, to repeat the French expression, again disgraced, and ordered to remain at his estate at Frésnes. He then gave great attention to general jurisprudence, and the branches of legislation immediately connected with it; to religion, and to the meditation of its sacred truths. To the hours thus spent by him, we owe the discourses on religious subjects, which fill the eleventh and twelfth volumes of the quarto edition of his works. All his biographers agree, that, in the course of his long life, he never let a day pass, without reading a portion of the Scriptures. In each of his removals from his office, he was aware of the cabals forming against him; he viewed them without emotion; he took no pains to counteract them; he returned to his station, without triumph, and without resentment.

He was recalled in 1727, and allowed to discharge the functions of his dignity; but the seals were not restored to him till after a period of ten years. He never regained the favour of the court; so that his recall was considered by the public as a necessary sacrifice, which the court unwillingly made to public opinion.

Throughout life, he preserved an attachment to polite literature and the exact sciences; they were his ornament in prosperity, his refuge in adverse fortune, the soother of his mind in the vexations and wearisomeness of professional and official duty, and the restoration of its energy, after fatigue, to new freshness and elasticity.

One day, he returned from his official duties, quite exhausted by exertion and fatigue. He immediately took up a mathematical work. At this, a friend of the chancellor, who chanced to be present, expressed great surprise, as it seemed to him to be adding fatigue to fatigue. "No;" said the chancellor, "a change of study has ever been to "me a relaxation."

The object nearest to his heart was to give

his children a good education, by impressing indelibly on their minds true principles of religion, virtue and honour. His unremitted attention to this important duty, edified and delighted all who witnessed it.

Like Cicero, whom he resembled in many other respects, he was fond of agriculture. His house was open to persons who excelled in literature or the arts, and it gave them pleasure to attend him. Viewing him in these occupations, persons might forget that he ever had any other. He frequently said that he engaged in these employments from pleasure, in his others, from duty; but when, after his banishments, he returned to his high offices, his temporary absences from them were not discoverable.

He was indefatigable in business; and, except conversation with men of taste, and a few hours occasionally given to literature, the change of employment was, to use his own expression, his sole recreation. He was abstemious, but lived in a manner suited to his high rank. Illustrious foreigners, who visited Paris, were received by him in a manner that did the nation and himself honour. He united in himself the characters of a profound lawyer, an accomplished magistrate, a skilful legislator, a man of science, and a polite scholar. In all the assemblies in which he presided, he listened with attention and deference; kept his superiority concealed as much as possible; and when he had to produce his own recondite learning and observations, did it without display. This rather enhanced than detracted from the merit of his discourses. To his brother magistrates he was always respectful; he took care that it should be observed that he relied on their wisdom and integrity. They were sensible of his attentions; they revered him as the ornament of their common profession, as their oracle. The advocates were equally attached to him; two of the greatest works, which French jurisprudence has produced, the "*Civil Law*" *of Domat* and the "*Pan-*" "*dectæ Justinianeæ*" *of Pothier*, received a marked encouragement from him. He assisted both the writers with his counsel: the letters, which passed between him and Pothier, are very interesting. Sometimes, however, according to the Duke de St. Simon, envy and jealousy of his superior talents and merit were discoverable.

He was highly respected by all men of letters; his biographers mention, that in the last year of his life, he was consulted by the learned of England, on the reformation of the Calendar, which was then in agitation.

CHAPTER THE SIXTH.

The Ordonnances framed by D'Aguesseau.

THE Chancellor's views of legislation shew both the solidity and elevation of his mind. His chief aim was to produce an uniformity of law throughout the kingdom of France, preserving as much of the established jurisprudence as was compatible with such an operation. To effect this purpose, he directed his attention successively to three objects, the laws themselves, the processes by which they were carried into execution, and the courts of justice.

He then proceeded to frame several ordonnances, and other judicial instruments, which were to carry his intentions into effect. They were afterwards duly signed by the King, and registered by the Parliament; then, they became laws of the State. We shall present our readers with a translation of the heads of them, inserted by M. Thomas, in the twelfth note to his Eloge of the Chancellor.

"For a long time," says M. Thomas, "the differences in the laws of France, and "the prodigious number and variety of cus-"toms prevailing in it, had been complained "of. It certainly was to be wished, that, as "the nation was governed by the same "prince, it should also be governed by the "same laws. But to effect this uniformity of "law, is one of those enterprizes, which strike "by their grandeur, but terrify by the diffi-"culties, which attend them. M. D'Agues-"seau, who, for a long time, had entertained "great views on the subject of legislation, at "length resolved to carry them into execu-"tion. His design was to establish a com-"plete uniformity in the administration of "the antient laws, without changing the "substance of them; but adding to them "what should be found necessary to render "them perfect. To execute properly this "object, he proposed to give his attention, "successively, to those cases which turned "on questions of law, those which related "to judicial process, and those which re-

" spected the jurisdiction and powers of the " courts. M. D'Aguesseau, notwithstanding " the extent of his own knowledge, thought " it would be wrong to trust to his own light. " He had too much capacity, not to have " recourse to the capacity of others. There- " fore, by a letter, equally full of eloquence " and solid reasoning, he announced his pro- " ject of legislation to all the sovereign courts " of France: he then sent them the mater " of each proposed law, in the form of ques- " tions. The courts caused their answers " to be prepared by advocates of cele- " brity, and honoured by the Chancellor's " choice. These were afterwards discussed by " the best informed members of the Parlia- " ment of Paris; and the Procureur Général " reported upon them, to the Chancellor. All " the papers were then transmitted to the " *Maîtres des Requêtes*. The law was finally " settled at the *Bureau de Législation*, at " which the Chancellor presided. It then re- " ceived the royal signature, and became a " law of the State. Thus it was, that one " man spread emulation and exertion through " all the body of the French magistracy.

" Every law was the work of all the most
" intelligent men in France.

1st. " The first appeared in April 1729.
" It revoked the celebrated edict of Saint
" Maur, and thereby, *mothers* were allowed
" to succeed to the real and personal estates
" of their children, who died without issue, in
" conformity to the dictates of nature, which
" were violated by that edict.*

2d. " A declaration of the King, of the
" 15th of January 1731,—respecting *primi-*
" *tive curates and perpetual vicars.* It en-
" abled them to recover by a short process
" the tithes provided for their subsistence.

3d. " A declaration of the 5th of February
" 1731:—By this, the rights of *Provostships*
" *and Presidials,* which had been carried to
" an extent dangerous to the subjects, were
" regulated by wise limitations.

4th. " In the same month of the same
" year,—the Ordonnance on *Donations* ap-
" peared. It enacted certain clear and sim-
" ple provisions for regulating this mode of
" disposing of property.

* Appendix, Note I, p. 79.

5th. "In August 1735,—the Ordonnance of *Testaments* established a just medium between an excessive indulgence of testamentary power, and the too rigorous restraint of it; and put an end to a diversity of jurisprudence on this important subject.

6th. "In July 1737,—the Ordonnance on *Falsification* threw light and order into the chaos, in which cases on this subject were involved, under the antient law.*

7th. "In August 1737,—an Ordonnance, on the *Citations and Summonses* of the judges, remedied the abuses, which had found a way into these preliminary proceedings, and lessened their length and expense.

8th. "In 1738,—the famous regulation respecting the mode of proceedings in the *Supreme Council* was promulgated: it reduced their length, delays, and expense.

9th. "In 1747,—the Ordonnance on *Substitutions* was promulgated: it shewed them the greatest degree of favour that

* Appendix, Note II, p. 80.

"they could or ought to receive: it put an "end to the interminable contestations upon "them; introducing into the laws respecting "them clear principles in the place of the "subtleties of the antient law.*

10th. "In August 1748,—the Ordonnance "respecting persons entitled to hold lands "in *mortmain* appeared. It allowed and "confirmed their right to the property then "so held; but inhibited such settlements of "it, in future.

11th. "In August 1749,—*several Royal* "*Courts of Justice in the same town*, and the "tribunals depending upon them, were con-"solidated into one court; by which, great "expense was saved to litigants."

All these laws regarded the *kingdom at large*, and had an universal operation over it in all its parts: D'Aguesseau was the author and framer of many *salutary laws, which had partial, but extensive effects.* One, in order to promote the growth of silk, made it penal to destroy the leaves of mulberry-trees. Another, regulated the exportation of corn. The

* Appendix, Note III, p. 80.

eulogists of D'Aguesseau proclaim this edict to have been so wisely framed, that it encouraged the exportation of corn till the very moment of its becoming injurious to the nation, and then made it cease.—We receive this account of it with some hesitation. When *Colbert* summoned some of the principal merchants of France to attend him, he courteously asked them, "what he could do to encourage "the commerce of France?" "Leave it to "itself,"—was their unanimous and only answer.

It should be added, that the Chancellor always had in his house a professional gentleman of consummate knowledge of the law, and great skill in business. He arranged and minuted the Chancellor's papers; and every morning laid before him a note of the business of the day. With this gentleman, D'Aguesseau discussed the matters, which came before him, and almost every subject of importance, in which he was concerned. This circumstance was mentioned to the writer by one of the venerable magistrates, whom the misfortunes of the times drove to this country at the commencement of the French Revolution:

he related it from his own knowledge; and added, that D'Aguesseau remunerated the services of this gentleman most liberally.

On the promulgation of an ordonnance, D'Aguesseau often caused a treatise to be prepared with great care, by some jurisconsult of known ability, which explained its object, and intended operation and effect. If, after all these cares, any grave person entertained a doubt of the wisdom or operation of the ordonnance, or of the right construction of it, D'Aguesseau was always ready to listen to him; he often answered such observations by letter.

By what has been stated, and still more by a perusal of the Ordonnances themselves, the reader will perceive the great deliberation, the profound and extensive knowledge of law, the vast researches, the numerous consultations and elaborate care, with which these ordonnances were framed.

They had been preceded by the celebrated *Ordonnance sur la Marine*, of M. Colbert,—a legislative enactment universally admired, and more or less adopted by every court of marine jurisdiction in Europe. The late Mr. Serjeant

Hill always mentioned in terms of the highest respect, the wisdom of the system it established, the lucid order of its provisions, and the clearness and precision of its language.

TO the honour of the English people, and we may add,—to the great increase of their happiness, we now, for the first time, possess, in *Mr. Peel's Five Acts* of Parliament,* a series of legislative enactments, of the highest importance and the most extensive operation, which in every kind of legislative merit, equal the Ordonnances we have mentioned. The obligations of the nation to Mr. Peel on this account are incalculable. His explicit declaration, of the great readiness, both of the highest and all other members of the legal profession, to cooperate with him in his noble and arduous undertaking to simplify the law, and lessen its expense and delay, reflects honour on them, and completely refutes the charge, too often brought against them, of a contrary spirit.

Highly also are we indebted to Mr. Peel, for *the Commissions, on the Common Law, the*

* 7 & 8 Geo. IV. c. 27, 28, 29, 30, 31.

Court of Chancery, and Real Property, which he has instituted. The Commissioners, and all whom they have examined, have exhibited the most earnest wish that the defects of the present system should be brought to view, and remedied by extensive and salutary reforms and improvements.

The two Reports of *the Common Law Commissioners* have given universal satisfaction: that of *the Chancery Commissioners* abounds with just and useful observations: it is signed by Lord Eldon, confessedly the highest legal authority, which the United Empire possesses: the *Real Property Commissioners* have published one Report, and promised another.

All the reports were preceded by Mr. Humphreys's profound, original, useful, and learned "*Observations on the actual state of* "*Real Property.*"

The *Ordonnances of the Chancellor D'Aguesseau*, and *Mr. Peel's Five Acts of the 7th and 8th of His present Majesty*, are framed on the same plan. They abrogate certain portions of the old law; adopt and enact others, and leave the rest untouched: these, therefore, continue in force; and all the written and unwritten law, both of the *enacted* and the *continued* portions of the old law, is preserved.

He was acting in conformity to the plan suggested and approved by Lord Bacon. "I dare not," said that great man, "advise "to cast the law into a new mould. The "work, which I propound, tendeth to pruning "and grafting the law: and not to ploughing "up and graiting it again: for such a re- "move I should hold indeed for a perilous "innovation."*

Some respectable jurisconsults assert, that a much greater reduction of the law of a country may be made by pursuing another plan. They contend, that the whole, both of its written, and unwritten law, may be abrogated; that a new CODE, sufficient for all the legal wants of the nation, may be formed in one volume, or in a few volumes of no great bulk, and contain *all* its law.

This is termed *Codification;* and the *Five Codes Napoléon* are referred to, as a proof of

* See his *Proposal for amending the Laws of England.*

the practicability of the scheme; of the excellent manner in which it can be executed; and of the salutary effects which such an execution of it is likely to produce.

Other jurisconsults, equally respectable, maintain a contrary opinion. They remark the acknowledged failure of *the Pandects*, which, after they were acted upon, produced insensibly as great an accumulation of laws, as that, which they were intended to supersede.

They admit the excellence of the Napoléon Codes; and that they have, in several respects, been highly beneficial to France; but, they argue, that it does not follow that, because such a measure was practicable by Napoléon in the prostrate and ravined condition, in which France and all its religious and civil institutions were found by him,—possessed too, as he was, of the most arbitrary, boundless and irresistible power ever attained by a sovereign,—the same, or a similar measure is equally practicable in states which are in possession of their antient governments and antient laws and institutions,—and must conform to them in all their operations.

They refer to the fates of the Prussian, Austrian, Bavarian and Russian codes.

They also suggest, that it cannot be said with accuracy, that where such a codification as that of Napoléon, is achieved, the code,—*and the code only*,—will thenceforth be the law of the land. Is there, they ask, an instance, in which this has taken place? Or an instance, in which the operation of the code has gone further, than to provide that its enactments shall have effect in all the cases, to which they extend; and to leave its other national jurisprudence in force,—with all its adjuncts of written and unwritten law?

This, they assert, is the actual state of the law of France. It evidently consists, by their representation of it,

1. Of the portions of the old law, which the *Codes Napoléon* have adopted and enacted:

2. Of the portions of the old law, upon which the *Codes Napoléon* have no operation, and which therefore are yet in force:

3. Of the new law:

4. Of the written and unwritten law, which made a part of, or was applicable to the *enacted* or *continued* portions of the old law:

5. Or, which is applicable to it by fair argument or inference:

6. And of the interpretation of the codes, which has taken place since their promulgation, and which will of course continue.

Every account from the continent seems to them to shew, that the bulk of the French law is yet very great; that it immeasurably exceeds the size of the codes; and that it is on the increase.

They also inform us, that the avocâts and jurisconsults on the continent are divided into two parties,—one, consisting of those, who wish the codes to bend to the old law; the other,—of those, who wish the old law to bend to the codes.

They cite a note in M. Tournier's edition and translation of Lord Bacon's "Universal Law," in which M. Tournier says, "that the "laws, which have been made in France "since the French Revolution, are only in-

"coherent heaps of articles mixed up to-"gether;" that, "they are comments, not "explanations; contradictions, not repeals; "references, not substitutions." He cites an author, "who assimilates them to an arsenal "furnishing arms to all parties, to all in-"terests, and to all sophisms." He states, that "a decree of the year 1813, (now "apparently wholly forgotten), ordered an "entire revision of the laws."*

* In the Case of Langdon *v.* Langdon, heard in the Court of Chancery on the 21st of April 1830, which arose on the construction of the 13th of the new Orders of Court,—the Lord Chancellor intimated, that "he "thought that Order not quite correctly worded, and "that the opinion of the other Equity Judges ought to "be obtained upon it." He said, it was "well known "that the *Code Napoléon,* which was so much boasted "of, was defective, and that a mass of decisions had "been collected upon it."

Morning Chronicle, 22d April 1830.

The writer takes this opportunity to mention, that he has made some attempts to procure exact information of the opinions entertained by French lawyers, of the authority of the *Codes Napoléon.* From his communications with them, he believes there is a great discrepancy of opinion on this head. He thinks the prevalent notion of the best informed is conformable to what he has intimated on the text. He believes the *code civil,*—to which almost exclusively his own attention has been called, is univer-

A number of similar testimonies might, they say, be easily collected. They particularly refer to the valuable information, respecting foreign jurisprudence, contained in the "*Lettres sur la Chancellerie d'Angleterre, et sur quelques points de la Jurisprudence Anglaise, par M. P. C. Cooper, avocât Anglais; et publiées avec une Introduction par M. P. Royer Collard, Avocât de la Cour Royale de Paris, et Professeur à la Faculté du Droit.*"

If it were desired to form a *Code of the Law of Contingent Remainders and Executory Devises*, it could not, perhaps, be done better, than by a statute, which should propound, in the form of a code, all the principles and rules of law laid down in Mr. Fearne's Essay, and declare them to be law. To acquire a knowledge of this code, would it be less necessary, after the enactment of the statute, to

sally admired: he has met French magistrates under the *ancien regime*, who hold the French revolution, and every thing connected with it, in abomination; who nevertheless spoke of the *code civil* in terms of the highest praise. His own esteem of it he mentions with great distrust, as repeated experience has shewn him, how very difficult it is for a lawyer of one country, to obtain any thing like an accurate knowledge of the law of another.

study the Essay, and the authorities on which it is founded, and to advise with the learned and experienced, than it is at present?

Since the preceding part of this work was written, we have seen the acts for amending the English law, brought into parliament by Sir Edward Burtenshaw Sugden, his Majesty's Solicitor-General, and universally approved. He will continue to deserve well of his country, by procuring other legislative acts equally salutary.

It is inconceivable, how much, in numerous points both of moment and frequent occurrence, the law of England is open to doubt. The cases of Doe *v.* Helder, and Doe *v.* Burdett, have thrown the law on outstanding estates and interests, of so much importance to the security of titles to real estate, into an uncertainty, that cries to heaven.

TO return to the Chancellor D'Aguesseau. The time spent by him in the formation of his ordonnances, never interfered with the discharge of his official duties, or withheld him from attending to cases of compassion, to which his attention was solicited. When the law furnished him with no means of granting the relief prayed for by the parties, he frequently relieved them from his own purse; carefully concealing it from the parties.

All the ordonnances and other judicial enactments framed by the chancellor D'Aguesseau, are inserted in the Ordonnances de Louis XV. published in one duodecimo volume.

CHAPTER THE SEVENTH.

Charge of refinement and dilatoriness brought against D'Aguesseau by the Duke de Saint-Simon.

THE Duke de Saint-Simon,* allows that the chancellor D'Aguesseau possessed, in the highest degree, genius, application, penetration, learning of every kind, magisterial gravity, equity, piety, purity of life, integrity, good nature, mildness, humanity, and candour in his public character: he says that in his private life, he was elegant, pleasing, and though very sober, very cheerful; that his manners were highly polished; his sentiments and conduct noble, and that he was wholly free from pride and avarice.

But all these great qualities were, according to the duke's representations, wholly undone by three qualities, which accompanied them,—his support of the parliament

* Memoirs, Vol. IX. p. 1.

against the crown,—his too great partiality to the members of his own profession,—and his too great refinement and slowness.

The first of these qualities will scarcely be thought a crime by an English reader; the second, could not often intervene. In respect to the third, we say with *Henrys*, who, in his time, was consulted as an oracle of law:—
" He, who judges too quickly, seems to run
" to repentance: judges should fear hasty
" decisions; they should recollect, that the
" greatest mistakes, which are found in the
" judgments of the courts, have proceeded
" from the impatience of the bench. To
" give full attention to advocates, and to
" allow them to speak without interruption,
" all the time they desire, is not so much an
" act of civility, as the performance of a
" duty." *

But D'Aguesseau himself was his own best apologist: his son once intimated to him, that he was accused of slowness. " My child," said the Chancellor, " when you shall have

* Cited from Dupin's Dissertation on the Life of Pothier, prefixed to the last edition of his Works.

"read what I have read, seen what I have "seen, and heard what I have heard, you "will feel, that if, on any subject you know "much, there yet may be something that "you do not know; and that something even "of what you know, may not, at the time, "be in your recollection: you will then, too, "be sensible of the mischievous and often "ruinous consequences of even a small error "in decision; conscience will then, I trust, "make you as doubtful, as timid, and con-"sequently as dilatory as I am accused of "being."

The Duke de Saint-Simon mentions that the Duke de Grammont on some occasion, asked the Chancellor D'Aguesseau, whether, with his experience of the chicanery of the law in legal process, and of the length of legal proceeding, he had never thought of some regulation, which might put an end to them. "I had gone so far," answered the Chancellor, "as to commit to writing a plan of "such a regulation; but, after I had made "some progress, I reflected on the great "number of advocates, attornies and officers, "whom it would ruin; compassion for them

" made the pen drop from my hand. The " length and number of lawsuits confer on " the gentlemen of the long robe, their wealth " and authority; one must therefore permit " their infant wealth and everlasting endur-" ance." The editor of the Duke de Saint-Simon's Memoirs shrewdly observes, that if a person should consider the immense sums, which in various forms, the crown receives from lawsuits, he would soon perceive, that lawyers are not the sole gainers by them; and consequently not the only persons interested in their preservation.*

It was sometimes objected to D'Aguesseau, that he consumed too much time in the company of men of letters. " But, no one," said D'Aguesseau, " can accuse me of giving too " much time to relaxation. And how can " I relax myself better than in the society of " men, whose taste and learning all the world " admires? they both instruct and delight " me."

It has been often said that D'Aguesseau intended to make the administration of the

* Œuvres de Saint-Simon, Tom. IX. p. 12.

law of France, gratuitous: it has been conjectured that he proposed to effect this by abolishing all law-taxes, and rendering it unnecessary for parties to appear in suits by attorney. From papers, which fell into the hands of the present writer, on the death of a person advised with by the ministry, who succeeded the Duke de Choiseuil, it appears that this project of D'Aguesseau was then taken up, and seriously considered.

CHAPTER THE EIGHTH.

Death of the Chancellor D'Aguesseau.

In the commencement of the year 1750, the Chancellor began to find himself unequal to the discharge of his duties. He resolved therefore to resign his high office, and wrote a letter to the King, requesting his permission for it. Having received this permission, he prepared the act of resignation; and, even in this document, shewed, according to all his biographers, great learning and knowledge of form. He then signed it. On the following day, he placed the seals in the hands of the Count of Saint Florentin. This count and the two sons of D'Aguesseau delivered them into the hands of Louis XV. The Monarch continued to D'Aguesseau the dignity and honours of the charge; and settled on him, during his life, a yearly pension of 100,000 livres,—about £.4800. of English money; but nearly double the amount of that sum, if we consider the relative value of money, at that time and the present.

From this time, the Chancellor dedicated himself entirely to a religious preparation for the awful passage into eternity. He died on the 9th of February 1751. That day was the last of the 83d year of his life.

He had married in 1694, Ann D'Ormesson, and survived her some years.

By his own desire, he was buried in the churchyard of his parish, under a simple cross. Louis XV. caused a magnificent mausoleum, in the form of an obelisk, to be erected to his memory; and a copy of the works of D'Aguesseau to be sent to the First President of each of the Parliaments of France, and some other principal magistrates. The monument was destroyed at the beginning of the French revolution, and afterwards restored at the public expense: in 1810, statues of D'Aguesseau and of the *Chancellor L'Hopital* were placed, in parallel positions, before the peristyle of the Palais Legislatif.

The works of the Chancellor D'Aguesseau were first published in thirteen volumes quarto; an improved edition of them has been since published in sixteen volumes, in octavo.

The most interesting portions of them, to an English reader, are, the Chancellor's Instructions to his Son for the study of the Law,—his Discourses on the Duties of Magistrates,—his Discourse on the Life and Decease of his Father,—and his Memoirs on the Ecclesiastical Concerns of France. The two first are inserted in the first volume of the quarto edition of his works; the two last in the thirteenth; but there are many other parts of his writings, which an English lawyer may read with pleasure and advantage. His "*Discourse on Mistakes of Law*," by persons executing deeds, or otherwise acting under those mistakes, has been translated by Mr. Evans, in the second volume of his translation of Pothier's celebrated "Treatise on the Law of Obligations and Contracts." This Discourse will be found worthy of the high character of D'Aguesseau.

The English magistrate, to whom the Chancellor D'Aguesseau may be best compared, is *Sir Matthew Hale*. The lives of both exhibit the same character, of modest, retiring, and religious virtue; the same indefatigable industry in the acquisition of judicial knowledge; the same pursuits of general literature and science; the same edifying discharge of official duty; the same profound erudition in all that related to the laws and constitution of their country; the same enlarged views of its jurisprudence; and the same zeal for its amelioration. Both left numerous works, in which learning, genius, and good sense appear in every page. Happy is the nation, on whom Providence bestows such magistrates! These equally benefit their own times and posterity.

APPENDIX.

APPENDIX.

NOTE I. *referred to in page* 53.

THE law of the *Ten Tables* entirely excluded females from inheritance: the *Prætorian* law partially admitted them to it; the *Tertullian senatus-consultum* opened it to mothers, who had acquired the *Jus trium liberorum*. *Justinian*, by his Novels, extended it generally to all mothers, but directed them to share it with the collaterals of the deceased. (See *Heineccius, Syntagma Antiquitatum Romanarum*, Lib. III. Tit. 1. 2. 3.)

The Ordonnance cited in the text refers to this state of the Roman law in the time of Justinian. It says, that the succession of mothers to their children, who died without issue, took place in every part of France, in which the civil law prevailed. It then mentions that Charles IX. by the Edict of Saint-Maur, in 1567, had deprived mothers of the succession, and allowed them only the income of the real estate of their deceased children during their lives; but permitted them to retain their right to the absolute property of the personal estate of their children. The Ordonnance then states, that this edict had been registered by the parliament of Paris, but that the provinces governed by the Roman Law had often petitioned for its repeal. It then revokes the Edict of Saint Maur: and directs that, for the future, successions should, in those parts of France, which were governed by the civil law, be regulated in the same manner, as if the Edict of Saint Maur had never existed.

Note II. *referred to in page* 54.

The preamble of this Ordonnance states that Louis XIV. had attempted to reduce all the laws respecting *Falsification* into one enactment; and had failed in the attempt. With a similar view, D'Aguesseau framed the Ordonnance now under consideration. It is divided into three titles: the first relates to what he terms *Falsifications principal;*—these are, when no suit respecting the instrument said to be falsified being then depending, the party institutes a suit, in which he asserts that the instrument complained of is falsified, and prays the court for a sentence declaring it to be so. The second respects what he terms *Falsifications incidental;*—these arise on instruments which have been brought into court during the progress of a cause. The third regards falsification on *Confession or acknowledgments* of writings or signatures in criminal causes. The first title contains sixty-nine articles; the second, fifty-three; the third, twenty-one. It is evidently a work of great labour; it is methodically arranged, and expressed with great precision and perspicuity.

Note III. *referred to in page* 55.

Probably none of the Ordonnances of the Chancellor D'Aguesseau, will interest an English reader so much, as that on *Substitutions.* We think a short mention, in this place, of the Roman, the Justinian, the antient French, the Nápoléon, and English jurisprudence respecting them, will not be unacceptable to our readers.

1. Nothing could be more simple than the *Roman law* of property, as it was settled by the *Trebellian and Pegasian decrees:* it was innovated by the introduction of

the *fidei-commissa*. These gave rise to successive fidei-commissary substitutions. By multiplying these, and by prohibiting each substitute from aliening the inheritance, property was absolutely taken out of commerce, and fixed in a settled and invariable course of devolution in particular families. There is reason to suppose this mode of settling property was never common.

2. The policy of *Justinian* soon interfered to check it. By the 159th Novel, he restrained fidei-commissary substitutions to four degrees, including the party himself, who instituted the substitutions. With the third substitute, therefore, the power of the testator expired; the absolute dominion vesting absolutely in the third substitute. This in some measure restored the law to its primitive simplicity.

3. A similar process is discoverable in the history of *French jurisprudence* respecting substitutions. For a long time, the law of France appears to have generally admitted perpetual substitutions. The Ordonnance of Orleans in 1560, restrained them to two degrees, exclusive of the instituant. That Ordonnance not having a clear operation, and the inconvenience arising from prior substitutions being greatly felt, the Ordonnance of Moulins in 1566, restrained all substitutions, anterior to that Ordonnance, to the fourth degree from the instituant. The Ordonnance of 1747, mentioned in the text, fixed the law on this important branch of property. It was evidently framed with great deliberation, by the Chancellor D'Aguesseau, after taking the sentiments of every Parliament in the kingdom, upon forty-five different questions proposed to them on the subject. These questions, and the answers of the Parliaments, have been published under the title, *Questions concernant les substitutions; Toulouse* 1770.

The Ordonnance of 1747 confines substitutions, with some exceptions, to two degrees; and directs the degrees to be computed by the individuals, in whom the substitutions should rest. Upon this, it was held, that, if the testator appointed several persons jointly to the inheritance, they formed together but one degree; if he appointed to it several persons successively, though in the same degree of kindred, as brothers or sisters, each person in whom the succession vested, formed one degree.

4. The *Code Napoléon*, by the article 896, prohibits substitutions altogether: but, by the articles 1048, 1049, and 1050, it allows parents to settle the property on any one or more of their sons or daughters; and, after their respective deceases, on their respective children; and also allows the parent, if he leave no child, to settle it on his own brothers and sisters, or any of them and their children, in the same manner; but the children of the sons and daughters, and also the children of the brothers and sisters, are to take equally and absolutely.

5. The judicial system of property received in *England*, is complicated; but it is perfect, both in theory and for practical objects. Every intelligent person must consider with admiration, how completely a marriage settlement or a will, when it is properly prepared, confers the beneficial ownership on the temporary possessor, for every legitimate purpose, while his abuse of it is prevented. He must also admire the good sense with which the present system of entailing property has been formed; which, while it provides for the perpetuation of a numerous and respectable aristocracy, leaves a sufficient proportion of land in commerce, to answer the demands of individuals, and to effectuate the general object of the national policy, that the owners of personal property should both have opportunities of realizing it, and be

allured to its realization by the superior stability of landed property, and the importance which the ownership of it confers.

This, it is known, has been effected by the establishment of a general rule, that the absolute ownership of property may be suspended from vesting in any one during the life of a person in being at the time of the creation of the entail, and a further period of twenty-one years, to be computed from his decease: but that at the end of this period, the entail shall cease of itself in some cases, and be barrable in others. The series of decisions, by which this salutary rule has been established, may be traced to the time of Charles II, and was not perfected till nearly the close of the last reign. However abstruse and complicated it may be, the system is coherent; the decisions, upon which it is founded, are countless; but they all converge to the same result,—an incontestable proof of the great good sense, the profound knowledge of law, and the mature deliberation, with which they have been framed.

AN

HISTORICAL AND LITERARY

ACCOUNT

OF THE

ROMAN AND CANON LAW.

FOURTH EDITION.

CONTENTS.

AN HISTORICAL AND LITERARY ACCOUNT OF THE ROMAN LAW.

AN HISTORICAL AND LITERARY ACCOUNT OF

THE CANON LAW.

V. 2. *The Middle Period of the Canon Law.*

APPENDIX.

HISTORICAL AND LITERARY ACCOUNT

OF

THE ROMAN LAW.

I.

THOSE, who wish to trace the ROMAN LAW to its origin, almost immediately find themselves obliged to form an opinion on a point which has been the subject of much discussion, and a decision upon which is not very easy, *the degree of credit due to the histories, which have reached us, of the five first ages of Rome.* The credibility of them was ingeniously attacked by M. de Pouilly, and as ingeniously defended by L'Abbé de Sallier, in their dissertations on this subject, in the Memoires de l'Academie. In his discourses *Sur l'incertitude des cinq premières siecles de l'Histoire Romaine,* M. de Beaufort seems to have determined the question. By a variety of arguments, drawn from the scantiness of the materials, from which these histories appear to have been framed, from the romantic nature of several of the exploits recorded in them, the improbability of many, the evident falsehood of some of their relations, and from the contradictions and absurdities, with which they frequently abound, he shews that, at least, where they descend into particulars, they should be read with a considerable degree of distrust. What they mention of the populousness of Rome, which, before the end of her second century, contained, by their accounts, 500,000 persons, appears incredible; but a smaller number would not have sufficed to construct the public works, with which, even then, Rome abounded. This circumstance has struck some modern writers so forcibly, that, to account for it, they have supposed, that Rome was raised on the ruins of a city, which, though now wholly forgotten, was once populous and magnificent, and the seat of a powerful empire. In pursuing this research, some have found such an empire among the Hetruscans. With the particulars of the history of that people, we are little acquainted; but we have certain information, that, long before the æra of the foundation of

Rome. they were a flourishing state, and excelled in arts and arms *

* See the Appendix to the Ancient Universal History, vol. 18. p. 187, and Maffei's Verona Illustrata, B. I. The expression of Livy, B. I. c. 2, is very strong, "Tanta opibus Etruria, ut jam non "terras solum, sed mare etiam per totam Italiæ "longitudinem, ab Alpibus ad fretum Siculum, "famâ nominis sui implesset." On the other hand, the silence of Herodotus may be thought a strong argument against the existence of such a city in his time.

II.

THE first object in the study of the Roman Law, is to obtain an accurate view of the LIMITS OF THE COUNTRIES, in which it prevailed, before the dismemberment of the empire. They may be divided into Italy, the conquests of the Romans in the other parts of Europe, and their conquests out of Europe.

II. 1. *Italy* is divided on the North, by the Alps, from France, Switzerland, and Germany; on every other side, it is washed by the Mediterranean. Its natural separation is into its northern, central, and southern divisions. Its northern division contains the modern Lombardy and the territories of Venice and Genoa, and reaches on every side to the Alps, from a line which may be supposed to be drawn from the Rubicon on the eastern, to the Macra on the western side of Italy.*

Its central division extends from the Rubicon to the Trento, near the Fortori, on the eastern sea, and from the Macra to the Silaro, on the western; and comprises Etruria, Umbria, Picenum, Sabinia, Latium, Lavinium, and Campania, or Tuscany, the Ecclesiastical State, and the Territory of Naples: its southern part contains the remainder of Italy, the Marsi, the Samnites, the Apulians, and the Lucanians. Before the Roman conquests of it, the northern division of Italy had been occupied by a colony of Gauls: on that account, it was known to the Romans, by the name of Gallia Cisalpina; and, from its being intersected by the Po, the northern division, made by that river, was called by them the Transpadanan, the southern was called the Cispadanan Gaul. The southern part of Italy

* See Appendix, Note I.

was peopled by colonies from Greece; on that account it was called Magna Græcia, by the Romans:—the part between Gallia Cisalpina and Magna Grecia, was called Italia Propria, or Proper Italy. The part of the Mediterranean, on the eastern side of the peninsula, was called the Higher, and afterwards the Hadriatic Sea; the part on its western side, was called the Lower or Tyrrhenean Sea.

With respect to its Antient State, it is probable, that the greatest part of Italy was in possession of the Hetruscans, when, about the year 964 before Christ, Evander arrived in Latium, and built a small town called Palantium. It is supposed, that Latinus reigned there, about the time of the Trojan war; that in his reign, Æneas landed in Italy, married Lavinia his daughter, and built Lavinium; that Ascanius, a son of Æneas, built Alba; that Romulus descended from him, and laid the foundation of Rome 753 years before Christ.

The monarchical government of Rome subsisted about 250 years; during the whole of this time, Rome was engaged in war with her neighbours; and perhaps the utmost extent of her conquests did not exceed a circumference of fifteen miles. In the next 250 years, the Romans conquered the remaining part of Italy, from the Alps to its southern extremity: then the conflict between her and Carthage commenced. From the destruction of Carthage, the æra of her foreign conquests may be dated; in the reign of Augustus, they reached the Atlantic, on the west; the Euphrates, on the east; the Rhine and the Danube, on the north; and Mount Atlas and the Cataracts of the Nile, on the south: under Domitian, they were carried to the Frith of Forth and the Clyde; and, under Trajan, over the Danube into Dacia, and over the Euphrates, into Mesopotamia and Armenia.

II. 2. *The European part of this spacious conquest* contained Hispania, or the kingdoms of Spain and Portugal:—Gaul, which comprised the whole country between the Pyrenees, the Ocean, the Rhine, and the Alps, or the present territory of France, with the addition of Switzerland:—Britannia, which comprised all England, Wales, and the lowland parts of Scotland, up to the Frith of

Forth and the Clyde: the Rhœtian and Vindelician provinces, which nearly comprised the Grisons, the Tyrolese, and a part of Bavaria :—the Norican, Pannonian and Dalmatian provinces, which, under the general name of Illyricum, filled the country between the Danube and the Hadriatic, up to ancient Greece—Mœsia, which comprised Servia and Bulgaria : — and Dacia, which comprised Temeswar and Transylvania, the only part of the Roman territory beyond the Danube; and Thrace, Macedonia, and Greece, the Roumelia of the Turks.

II. 3. *The Roman conquests out of Europe* reached over Minor Asia, Syria, Phenicia, and Palestine; over Ægypt, as far as Syene; and over the whole northern frontier of Africa. It should be added, that the countries on the northern shores of the Euxine, from the Danube on the west to Trebizond on the east, were tributary to the Romans, received their kings from Rome, and had Roman garrisons.*

* This article is chiefly extracted from the second chapter of the first volume of Mr. Gibbon's History; the geography of that work is unquestionably entitled to the highest praise.

III.

These were the limits of the Roman Empire; her subjects may be classed under the following divisions.

III. 1. The highest class of subjects was that of Roman citizens, or those who had the *Jus Civitatis.*

At a distance of about fourteen miles from the sea, the city of Rome stands on a cluster of small hills, contiguous to each other, rising out of an extensive plain, washed by the Tiber. At first, it was confined to the Palatine Hill; the Capitol was added to it by Titus Tatius; the Quirinal, by Numa; the Celian, by Tullus Hostilius; the Aventine, by Ancus Martius; and the Viminal and Esquinal by Servius Tullius. The city was surrounded by a wall; a slip of ground, on each side of it, was called the Pomœrium; the walls and Pomœrium were sacred: whoever extended the limits of the empire, had a right to extend the walls of the city; its last and greatest extension, was in the time of the Emperor Aurelian: he inclosed the Mons Pincius and Campus Martius within its walls. In 850,

Pope Leo added to it the Mons Vaticanus. At first, it was divided into four districts or regions; Augustus divided them into fourteen; modern Rome is divided into the same number; but the sites of the antient and modern districts or regions, considerably differ.

At first, all who fixed their residence in any part of the Roman territory, had the Jus Civitatis, or the rights of Roman citizens: afterwards the Jus Civitatis was conferred on few, and generally with limitations; in the course of time, it was granted to all of the Latin name. After the civil war, it was conferred on all the inhabitants of Italy, south of the Rubicon and Lucca: then it was granted to the Cisalpine Gaul, which, from this circumstance, was called Gallia Togata: finally, Caracalla communicated it to all the inhabitants of the Roman world.

The Jus Civitatis attached to those, who possessed it, the public rights and obligations attending the census, or enrolment in the censors' books; the Militia, or serving in the army; the Tributa, or taxation; the Suffragium, or voting in the different assemblies of the people; the Honores, or public offices of the state; and the Sacra, or a participation in the sacred rites of the city: it conferred on them the private rights and obligations of liberty, family, marriage, parental authority, legal property, making a will, succeeding to an inheritance, and tutelage or wardship.

The citizens of Rome were divided into Patricians or nobles, and Plebeians or inferior persons, and the middle order, called the Equites. At an immeasurable distance beneath the Plebeians, were the Slaves: their masters might set them free, they were then called freed-men; but, even after they were set free, their masters retained some rights over them.

The Romans were divided into gentes or clans; their clans into families; their families into individuals. Each individual had a prænomen, by which he was distinguished from others; a nomen, which denoted his clan; and a cognomen, which denoted his family; sometimes an agnomen was added, to denote the branch of the family to which he belonged. Thus, in respect to Aulus Virginius Tricostus Cœlimontanus,—Aulus, the prænomen, denoted the individual; Virginius, the nomen gentilitium, denoted, that he was of the Virginian clan; Tricostus, the cognomen, denoted, that he was of the Tricostan family of that clan; and Cœlimontanus, the agnomen, denoted, that he was of the Cœlimontan branch of that family: sometimes a further name was acquired, as Cunctator by Fabius, and Africanus by Scipio, in consequence of an illustrious deed.

III. 2. Next to the citizens of Rome, were the Latins, or those who had the *Jus Latii.* Antient Latium contained the Albani, Rutuli, and Æqui; it was afterwards extended to the Osci, Ausones, and Volsci: the difference between the right of the city and the right of Latium, is not precisely ascertained: the principal privilege of the Latins seems to have been, the use of their own laws, and their not being subject to the edicts of the Prætor; and that they had occasional access to the freedom of Rome, and a participation in her sacred rites.

III. 3. The Italians, or those who had the *Jus Italicum,* followed. All the country, except Latium, between the Tuscan and Hadriatic seas, to the rivers Rubicon and Macra, was, in this sense of the word, called Italy; the Italians had not access to the freedom of Rome, and did not participate in her sacred rites; in other respects, they were nearly on a footing with the Latins.

III. 4. Those countries were called *Provinces*, which the Romans had conquered, or in any other way, reduced to their power, and which were governed by magistrates, sent from Rome. The foreign towns, which obtained the rights of Roman citizens, were called *Municipia*. The cities or lands, which the Romans were sent to inhabit, were called *Coloniæ;* some consisted of Citizens, some of Latins, and some of Italians, and had therefore different rights.

Præfecturæ, were conquered towns, governed by an officer called a Præfect, who was chosen in some instances by the people, in others by the Prætors.

Civitates Fœderatæ, were towns in alliance with Rome, and considered to be free. All who were not Citizens, Latins, or Italians, were called *Peregrini* or foreigners; they enjoyed none of the privileges of Citizens, Latins, or Italians.*

* This article is extracted from the first Appendix to *Heineccius's Antiquitatum Romanarum Syntagma;* and, *Gravina's work, De Ortu et progressu Juris Civilis,* and his *Liber singularis de Romano Imperio:*—it will be found difficult to mention many works, which a practical lawyer, who wishes to relieve his mind from his professional labours by the perusal of a work of taste, on a subject connected with them, will read with so much pleasure as these three treatises:—and from *Spanheim's Orbis Romanus.*

IV.

SUCH were the limits of the Roman empire, and the different classes of Roman subjects;—with respect to its GOVERNMENT AND FORM OF LEGISLATION:

The ROMAN LAW, in the most extensive import of those words, denotes the system of jurisprudence, by which the Roman empire was governed, from its first foundation by Romulus, to its final subversion in the East, in consequence of the taking of Constantinople by Mahomet II. THE CIVIL LAW denotes that part of the Roman Law, which consists of the body of law compiled by the orders of the Emperor Justinian, and of the laws subsequently enacted by him, and called his Novells.

The writers on the History of the Roman Law, generally divide it into three æras,—the Jurisprudentia Antiqua, Media, and Nova. The first commences with the foundation of Rome, and extends to the æra of the Twelve Tables; the second extends to the reign of the emperor Adrian; the third to the reign of the emperor Justinian.

IV. 1. *As it was constituted by Romulus*, the Roman government consisted of an elective King; a Senate or Council, first of one hundred, and afterwards of two hundred nobles; and a general assembly of the people. The command of the army, the administration of justice, the superintendence of religious concerns, with the office of high priest, belonged to the King; the Senate deliberated on all public business, and prepared it for the people; to them, the right of final determination upon it belonged. The number of Senators was successively increased, to three hundred, by Tarquinius Priscus; to six hundred by Sylla; to nine hundred by Julius Cæsar; Augustus reduced it to six hundred. That, during the monarchy, the King had the right of appointing the Senators, is clear: how they were chosen during the æra of the republic, has been the subject of much dispute: some, with M. de Vertot, M. de Beaufort, and Lord Hervey, contend, that, as the Consuls succeeded to the royal power, they enjoyed the prerogative of filling up the Senate, till the creation of the Censors, to whom it then devolved: others, with Dr. Middleton, and Dr. Chapman, contend that the Kings, Consuls, and Censors, only acted in these elections, ministerially and subordinately to the supreme will of the people; with whom the proper and absolute power of creating Senators always resided.

The people were divided by Romulus into three Tribes, and each tribe into three Curiæ. Their public assemblies were called the *Comitia Curiata:* every member had an equal right of voting at them; and the votes were reckoned by the head. Thus, the issue of all deliberations depended on the poor, as they formed the most numerous portion of the community. To remedy this, Servius Tullius, the sixth King, divided the people into six classes, according to a valuation of their estates, and then subdivided the classes into an hundred and ninety-three centuries, and threw ninety-eight of the centuries into the first class; twenty-two, into the second; twenty, into the third; twenty-two, into the fourth; thirty, into the fifth; and the remaining part of the citizens into the sixth. The first class consisted of the richest citizens; the others followed in a proportion of wealth; the sixth consisted wholly of the poorest citizens. Each century, except the last, was obliged to furnish an hundred men in the time of war; the sixth was exempt from all taxes; and, to compensate this privilege to the rich, Servius enacted that, in the assemblies of the people, they should no longer count the votes by head, but by centuries, and that the first century should have the first vote. This arrangement, while it seemed to give every citizen an equal right of suffrage, as all voted in their respective centuries, virtually gave the richer classes the sole authority: but it was generally acceptable, as it conferred power on the rich, and immunity from taxes and the other burdens of the state, on the poor. These assemblies were called the *Comitia Centuriata.* For some purposes, however, particularly for the choice of inferior magistrates, and, in the time of the republic, for vesting military power in the Dictator, the Consuls, and the Prætors, the Comitia Curiata continued necessary.

On the expulsion of the last Tarquin, the Senate seems to have been permitted to retain, for some time, the constitutional power, under the regal state, of the monarchs whom they had dethroned: and to have used all means within their reach to perpetuate it in themselves.—During this period, the form of Roman legislation appears to have been, 1st, that the Senate should convene the Assembly, whether of Curiæ, or Centuriæ; 2dly, that the Consul should propound to them the matter to be discussed; 3dly, that the Augur should observe the omens, and declare whether they were favourable or unfavourable;—in the last case the Assembly was dissolved; 4thly, that the Assembly should vote; 5thly, that the Consul should report the resolution of the people to the Senate; and, 6thly, that the Senate should confirm or reject it.

IV. 2. These were the rights of the Consuls, the Senate, and the people, at the commencement of the republic; *several alterations successively took place*, in favour of the people, at the expense of the Consuls and the Senate.

With respect to the *Consuls*, their dignity and power were, by degrees, parcelled out among various magistrates:—thus the power of deciding in civil matters was assigned to the Prætors; their power of setting criminal prosecutions on foot was assigned to the Public Accusers; their care of the police, to the Ædiles; their general superintendence of morals and manners, to the Censors. After this, little more remained to the Consuls, than their right to assemble the Senate, convene the Comitia, and command the armies of the republic. The Consuls and higher magistrates were chosen by the people; at first, their choice was confined to the Patrician order; after much contest, it was extended to the people.

The influence of the patricians on the deliberations of the Comitia Centuriata was soon thought a grievance by the people: hence, upon every occasion which offered, they endeavoured to bring the business before the Comitia Curiata: but with this, they were not satisfied; for, as a patrician magistrate only could preside at the Comitia Curiata, and before the assembly proceeded to business, the omens were to be consulted, and none but patricians were admitted to the rank of Augur, the Comitia Curiata, though in a less degree than the Comitia Centuriata, were still subject to Patrician influence. To make the people entirely independent of the Patricians, at their general assemblies, the Tribunes insisted, that the public deliberations should be brought before the assemblies of the tribes, at which every Roman citizen had an equal right to vote, and at which neither the presence of a magistrate, nor the taking of the omens was essential. To this, the Senate and Patricians found it necessary to submit. At first, they contended, that they were not bound by the laws passed at these assemblies; but they were soon forced to acknowledge their authority. These assemblies were called the *Comitia Tributa.*

Some important privileges, however, still remained to the *Senate:* they had the direction of all concerns of religion, the appointment of ambassadors, of governors of the provinces, of the generals and superior officers of the army, the management of the treasury, and, speaking generally, they had the direction of all the religious, civil, and military concerns of the state, subject to the controul of the people, and subject also to the controul of any tribune of the people, who, by his *Veto*, might, at any time, prevent the resolution of the Senate from passing into a decree: but, when the people did not interfere, the Senatus-Consulta generally were obeyed; and it seldom happened that, in matters of weight, the people enacted a law, without the authority of the Senate. Thus the constitutional language of antient Rome was, that the Senate should decree, and the People order. By the senators themselves, it was deemed an heinous offence, that any of their body, without their leave, should propose a measure to the people: but, in the decline of the Republic, the leading men of Rome, and their creatures, paid no attention to this notion, and frequently obtained from the people, what they knew would be refused them by the Senate. The writings of Cicero abound with complaints against this practice. The determination of the people, at the Comitia Centuriata, Comitia Curiata, or Comitia Tributa, was equally *Lex*, or a law of the state; but when it passed in the Comitia Tributa, as it originated with the people, it was called *Plebiscitum:* the decrees of the Senate, were called *Senatus-Consulta.*

IV. 3. *The laws were distinguished*, sometimes by the name of the person who proposed them, as the law Æmilia: sometimes, by the names of the Consuls, if they were proposed by both the Consuls, as the law Papia Poppæa; and sometimes, a mention of the nature of the law was added, as the Lex Fannia Sumptuaria.*

* See *M. de Beaufort, La République Romaine; Paris* 1767, 6 *vols. 8vo. Letters between Lord Hervey and Dr. Middleton, concerning the Roman Senate; London* 1778, *4to.; and the* 12th, 13th, 14th, *and* 15th *Chapters of Montesquieu, l.* 11.

V.

For obtaining an exact view of the HISTORY OF THE ROMAN LAW, it may be divided into ten periods, severally beginning with the following epochs; 1st, the foundation of Rome; 2d, the Twelve Tables; 3d, the abolition of the Decemvirs; 4th, the reign of Augustus; 5th, the reign of Hadrian; 6th, the reign of Constantine the Great; 7th, the reign of Theodosius the Second; 8th, the reign of Justinian; 9th, the reign of his successors, till the fall of the Empire of the East; and 10th, the revival of the study of the civil law, in consequence of the discovery of the Pandects at Amalphi. A short view will then be taken of the principal schools in which the civil law has been taught, and of its influence on the jurisprudence of the modern States of Europe.

Before Christ.	Anno Urbis Conditæ.

V. 1.

V. 1. The FIRST OF THESE PERIODS contains the state of Roman jurisprudence from the foundation of Rome, till the æra of the Twelve Tables. 753 1

	Before Christ.	Anno Urbis Conditæ.
As Rome was a colony from Alba, it is probable that her laws originated in that city. Several of them are actually traced to her first kings; particular mention is made of laws enacted by Romulus, Numa, and Servius Tullius. Historians ascribe to Romulus the primitive laws of the Romans, respecting marriage, the power of the father over his child, and the relation between patron and client: to Numa, their primitive laws respecting property, religion, and intercourse with foreign states; to Servius Tullius, their primitive laws respecting contracts and obligations. It is supposed that, in the reign of the last of these kings, a collection of their laws was promulgated by public authority. The scanty materials which have reached us, of the regal jurisprudence of Rome, lead to a conjecture that the Romans had attained a high degree of legislative refinement before the abolition of royalty.		
Tarquin, the last King of Rome, was expelled in	509	245

Before Christ.	Anno Urbis Conditæ.

Not long before or after his expulsion, a body of the Roman law, as it then stood, was collected by Papyrius, and from him was called, *Jus Civile Papyrianum*. The president Terasson, (*Histoire de la Jurisprudence Romaine*, Paris, 1750, in folio, p. 22 & 73,) professes to restore the original of this compilation, as far as the materials which have reached us, allow: he has given us thirty-six laws,—fifteen of them as original texts, and twenty-one as the substance or sense of texts which are lost.

V. 2.

THE SECOND PERIOD OF THE HISTORY OF THE ROMAN LAW, is the æra of the Twelve Tables.

During the first half century which followed the expulsion of the Tarquins, the civil government of the Romans was in great confusion: on their expulsion, much of the antient law was abrogated, or fell into disuse, and some new laws were enacted by the Consuls.

	Before Christ.	Anno Urbis Conditæ.
The arbitrary and undefined power of the Consuls, in framing laws, growing very odious, three persons were sent into Greece, and probably to some of the most civilized states of Magna Grecia or Lower Italy, to obtain copies of their laws and civil institutions.	453	301
They returned in the third year after their mission. Ten persons, called from their number Decemvirs, were then appointed to form a code of law for the government of the state, both in private and public concerns. This they effected, and divided their code into ten distinct tables: two were added to them in the following year. They were a mixture of the laws of other nations, and of the old Roman law, adapted to the actual circumstances of the state of the people . .	451	303

They were inscribed on twelve tablets of brass; and, from that circumstance, were called the *Laws of the Tweve Tables.* The twelve tablets were exposed to the view of every person, in a public part of the market-place. In the sack of Rome, by the Gauls, they perished: immediately after the expulsion of the Gauls, their authority was restored, and the whole text of them was extant in the time of Justinian: fragments only of them have reached us. Gothofred's edition of these fragments, in his work intituled *Fontes Quatuor Juris Civilis*, Geneva 1653, in octavo, has obtained the universal applause of the learned: the fragments of them have also been published by the president Terasson; and Pothier has inserted them in his *Pandectæ Justinianeæ*, with an interpretation, and an excellent commentary.

The legislative wisdom of the Twelve Tables has been highly praised; but it has been thought, in some instances, immoderately severe. Thus, in respect to an insolvent debtor,—after the debt was proved or admitted, they allowed him thirty days to raise the money, or find surety for its payment: at the end of the thirty days, the law delivered him into the power of his creditor, who might confine him for sixty days in a private prison, with a chain of fifteen pounds weight, on a daily allowance of one pound of rice: during the sixty days, he was to be thrice exposed in the market-place, to raise the compassion of his countrymen: at the end of sixty days, if he was sued by a single creditor, the creditor might sell him for a slave beyond the Tyber; if he was sued by several, they might put him to death, and divide his limbs among them, according to the amount of their several debts.' Nothing can be urged in defence of this savage provision, if, as appears to be its true construction, the division, which it directs to be made, is to be understood literally of the body, and not of the price of the debtor: but if, before the Twelve Tables, an insolvent debtor became the slave of the creditor, so that his liberty and life were immediately in the power of the creditor, the ultimate severity of the provisions of the Twelve Tables should be ascribed to the harsh spirit of the people, and the intermediate delays in favour of the debtor should be ascribed to the humane policy of the Decemvirs. It may be added, that about two hundred years afterwards, the Petilian law provided that the goods, and not the body of the debtor, should be liable to his creditor's demands; and that, at a subsequent period, the Julian law provided, in favour of the creditor, the Cessio Bonorum, by which the debtor, on making over his property to his creditors, was wholly liberated from their demands. Upon the whole, if we consider the state of society, for which the laws of the Twelve Tables were formed, we shall find reason to admit both their wisdom and their humanity.

The journey of the Decemvirs into Greece has been questioned by M. Bonamy, *Mem. de l'Academie*, vol. xii. p. 27, 51, 75; and his doubts have been adopted by Mr. Gibbon; but the fact is either related or alluded to by almost every Roman author, whose works have come down to us: and some writers have professed to track the jurisprudence of Greece, even in the legislative provisions of the Prætors, Consuls, and Emperors.

V. 3.

V. In proportion as Rome increased in arms, arts, and the number of her citizens, the insufficiency of the laws of the Twelve Tables was felt, and new laws were passed. This insensibly produced, during the remaining part of the period of the republic, which forms THE THIRD PERIOD OF THE HISTORY OF THE ROMAN LAW, that immense collection of laws, from which the civil law, as the Justinianean body of law is called, was extracted, and which, on that account, deserves particular consideration.

It was divided, like the law of Greece, into the written and unwritten law. The written comprehended the Leges, Plebiscita, and Senatus-Consulta, which have been mentioned.

1. The first, and most important branch of the unwritten law of Rome was the *Jus Honorarium*, the principal part of which was the *Edictum Prætoris*. During the regal government of Rome, the administration of justice belonged to the king; on the establishment of the republic, it devolved to the Consuls, and from them, to the Prætor. At first, there was but one Prætor; afterwards, their number was increased to two; the Prætor Urbanus, who administered justice among citizens only; and the Prætor Peregrinus, who administered justice between citizens and foreigners, or foreigners only: the number of Prætors was afterwards increased, for the

administration of justice in the provinces and colonies. When the Prætor entered on his office, he published an edict, or system of rules, according to which he professed to administer justice for that year. In consequence of his often altering his edicts, in the course of the year, laws were passed, which enjoined him not to deviate from the form, which he should prescribe to himself, at the beginning of his office. All magistrates who held the offices, which were ranked among the honours of the state, had the same right of publishing edicts; and, on this account, that branch of the law, which was composed of the edict of the Prætor, and the edicts of those other magistrates, was called the *Jus Honorarium:* but the edicts of the Prætor formed by far the most important part of this branch of the Roman law. Such were his rank and authority in Rome, and such the influence of his decisions on Roman jurisprudence, that several writers on the Roman law mention his edicts in terms, which seem to import that he possessed legislative, as well as judicial power; and make it difficult to describe with accuracy, what is to be understood by the Prætor's edict. Perhaps the following remarks on this subject will be found of use, and shew an analogy between some parts of the law, of which the honorary law of Rome was composed, and some important branches of the law of England.—1st. By the Prætor's edict, as those words apply to the subject now under consideration, civilians do not refer to a particular edict, but use the words to denote that general body of law, to which the edicts of the Prætors gave rise.—2dly. It is to be observed, that the legislative acts of any state, form a very small proportion of its laws: a much greater proportion of them consists of that explanation of the general body of the national law, which is to be collected from the decisions of its courts of judicature, and which has, therefore, the appearance of being framed by the courts. A considerable part of the law, distinguished by the name of the Prætor's edict, was of the last kind; and, as it was a consequence of his decisions, received the general name of his law. In this respect, the legal policy of England is not unlike that of Rome; for, voluminous as is the statute book of England, the mass of law it contains bears no proportion to that, which lies scattered in the volumes of reports, which fill the shelves of an English lawyer's library: and perhaps it would be difficult to find, in any edict of a Prætor, a more direct contradiction of the established law of the land, than the decisions of the English judges, which, in direct opposition to the spirit and language of the Statute de Donis, supported the effect of common recoveries in barring estates tail.—3dly. Experience shews, that the provisions of law, on account of the general terms, in which they are expressed, or the generality of the subjects to which they are applicable, have frequently an injurious operation in particular cases, and that circumstances frequently arise, for which the law has made no provision. To remedy these inconveniences, the courts of judicature of most countries, which have attained a certain degree of political refinement, have assumed to themselves a right of administering justice in particular instances, by certain equitable principles, which they think more likely to answer the general ends of justice, than a rigid adherence to law; and, where law is silent, to supply its defects by provisions of their own. These privileges were allowed the Prætor by the law of Rome; in virtue of them, he pronounced decrees, the general object of which had sometimes a corrective, and sometimes a suppletory operation on the subsisting laws. They were innovations: but it may be questioned, whether any part of the Prætor's law was a greater innovation on the subsisting jurisprudence of the country, than the decisions of English courts of equity on the statute of frauds.—4thly. The laws of every country allow its courts a considerable degree of power and discretion in regulating the forms of their proceedings, and carrying them into effect; further than this, the Prætor's power of publishing an edict, signifying the rules by which he intended the proceedings of his courts should be directed, does not appear to have extended.—These observations may serve to explain the nature of the Prætor's jurisdiction, and to shew that the exercise of his judicial authority was not so extravagant or irregular as it has sometimes been described.*

2. A second source of the unwritten law of Rome was, the *Actiones Legis*, and *Solemnes Legum Formulæ*, or the Actions at Law, and Forms of Forensic proceedings, and of transacting legal acts. These, for some time, were kept a profound secret by the Patricians; but, Appius Claudius having made a collection of them for his private use, it was published by Cnæus Flavius, his secretary. The Patricians then devised new forms, and those were made public by Sextus Ælius. These publications were called the Flavian and Ælian Collections; all we have of them is to be found in Brisson's celebrated work, *De Formulis et Solemnibus Populi Romani Verbis.*

3. A third source of the unwritten law of Rome was derived from the *Disputationes Fori*, and the *Responsa Prudentum.* Mention has been made of the relation introduced by Romulus between patron and client;—to give his client legal advice, was among the duties

* See Appendix, Note II. p. 80.

of the patron; insensibly, it became a general practice, that those, who wanted legal assistance, should apply for it to the persons of whose legal skill they had the greatest opinion. This was the origin of the Jurisconsulti or Civilians of Rome; they were, generally, of the Patrician order; and, from succeeding to this branch of the duty of patronage, received the name of patrons, while those, by whom they were consulted, were called clients. The patron received his client with a solemnity bordering on magisterial dignity; and generally delivered, in a few words, his opinion on the case which was submitted to his consideration; but he sometimes accompanied it with his reasons. These consultations usually took place at an early hour in the morning: the broken slumbers of the Civilians are mentioned by every Roman poet, whose Muse has led him to describe the inconveniences which attend distinction and fame. Legal topics were often subjects of the conversations of Civilians; and the forum, from their frequent resort to it, being the usual scene of these friendly disputations, gave its name to them. They also published treatises on legal subjects. Their opinions and legal doctrines were highly respected; but, till they were ratified by a judicial decision, they had no other weight than what they derived from the degree of public estimation, in which the persons who delivered them were held. The Civilians are commonly divided into three classes; those, who flourished between the æra of the Twelve Tables, and the age of Cicero; those who flourished from the age of Cicero, to the reign of Severus Alexander; and those who flourished from the beginning of his reign, to that of the Emperor Justinian. The second, is the golden period of Antejustinianean jurisprudence. From the fragments which have reached us, of the opinions of the Civilians who flourished during that period, modern writers have thought themselves justified in describing them as men of enlarged minds, highly cultivated understandings, and great modesty.—In their judicial studies, they availed themselves of the learning and philosophy of the Greeks, carried the disputes of the schools of Athens into the Forum; and, early in the period of which we are speaking, branched into two sects, whose opposite tenets were founded on principles, not unlike those, which gave rise to the distinctive doctrines of the disciples of Zeno and Epicurus. Antistius Labeo was the founder of the former sect; Ateius Capito, of the latter: from Proculus and Pegasus, two eminent followers of Labeo, the former were called Proculeians or Pegasians; from Masurius Sabinius and Casius Longinus, two eminent followers of Capito, the latter were called Sabinians or Cassians. The former contended for a strict adherence to the letter and forms of the law; the latter for a benign interpretation of it, and for allowing great latitude in the observance of its forms. Attempts were made to compromise the difference between them: they gave rise to a third sect, the Juriscon sulti Erciscundi, or Miscalliones. Something of the difference which subsisted between the disciples of Labeo and Capito, has long subsisted in the jurisprudence of England; but the good sense of the English bar has prevented the maintainers of the different opinions from forming themselves into sects. Till the reign of Augustus, every person was at liberty to deliver judicial opinions; Augustus confined this privilege to particular persons, with a view, it is supposed, of their propagating those doctrines of law, which were favourable to his political system: the Emperor Adrian restored the general liberty: the Emperor Severus Alexander assigned it the limits within which it had been circumscribed by Augustus.

These are the materials of which the written and unwritten law of Rome was principally formed.

V. 4.

THE FOURTH PERIOD OF THE HISTORY OF THE ROMAN LAW, is that, which fills the space between the time when Julius Cæsar was made perpetual Dictator, and the reign of the Emperor Adrian. Before Christ. Anno Urbis Conditæ.
The power of Julius 46 708
Cæsar, in consequence of his perpetual dictatorship, placed him above law; but it does not appear that he made many innovations, of a general nature, in the Roman jurisprudence. That was left to Augustus, his heir and successor.

	Before Christ.	Anno Urbis Conditæ.

At different periods of his reign, the people conferred on Augustus the various titles of perpetual Tribune, Consul, Proconsul, Censor, Augur, and High Priest: thus, in effect, he acquired both the civil and military power of the state: but, as he professed to exercise it in virtue of those offices, his acts had the appearance of being the acts of the different magistrates, whose offices had been conferred on him. Finally, in the year of the city, 735, power was given him to amend or make whatever laws he should think proper. This was the completion of the *Lex Regia*, or of those successive laws, which, while they permitted much of the outward form of the republic to remain, invested the Emperor with absolute power. 16 | 735

During the whole of the reign of Augustus, the forms of the Leges and Senatus-consulta, those vestiges of dying liberty, as they are called by Tacitus, were preserved.

For the Senate, Augustus uniformly professed the greatest deference; he attended their meetings, seemed to encourage their free discussion of every subject, which came before them; and, when a law was approved of by them, he permitted it, agreeably to the antient forms of the republic, to be referred to the people. The reference of laws to the people was abolished by Tiberius; so that, from his time, the laws of Rome originated and were completed in the senate. At first, their deliberations had an appearance of free discussion; by degrees, even that vanished, and insensibly the Senate served for little more than a nominal council of the Emperor, an office to register his ordinances, and a court of judicature for great public causes.

V. 5.

THIS memorable revolution in the functions of the Senate, with which even the forms of Roman liberty expired, must be dated from the Emperor Adrian, and forms the FIFTH PERIOD OF THE HISTORY OF THE ROMAN LAW. He was the first of the Emperors, who exercised, without disguise, the plenitude of legislative power. With him, therefore, the *Imperial Constitutions*, under the various names of Rescripta, Epistolæ, Decreta, Edicta, Pragmaticæ Sanctiones, Orationes and Annotationes, originated; they had the force of law in every part of the Roman state. Under his reign, Julian, a lawyer of great eminence, digested the Prætor's edicts, and other parts of the Jus Honorarium, into a regular system of law, in fifty books. This compilation was much esteemed; it was referred to as authority, and obtained the title of *Edictum Perpetuum*. All the remains of it, which have come down to us, are the extracts of it in the digest; they have been collected with great attention, by Simon Van Leeuwen, at the head of the Digest, in his edition of Gothofred's Corpus Juris Civilis, Lugd. Batav. 1663 120

After Christ.

It was a remarkable effect of the Edictum Perpetuum, to put an end to the legal schism of the Sabinians and Proculians. By countenancing the former, in the Edictum Perpetuum, the Emperor Adrian terminated the dispute.

The Institutes of Gaius, an illustrious lawyer in the reign of the Antonines, after having long existed only in an imperfect abridgment, have been recently discovered and published.* After Christ.

After this, came the *Codex Gregorianus;* a collection of Imperial constitutions, from Adrian to Dioclesian, by Gregorius or Gregorianus, Prætorian Præfect to Constantine the Great 284

This was succeeded by the *Codex Hermogenianus*, a continuation of the former code, by Hermogenes, a contemporary of Gregorius or Gregorianus.†

V. 6.

THE SIXTH PERIOD OF THE ROMAN LAW extends from the reign of Constantine the Great, to that of the

* See *Mr. Irwin's excellent Observations on the Study of the Civil Law*, 3d ed. pp. 48, 49, 50.

The first volume of the *Themis ou Bibliothèque des Jurisconsults* contains an abridgment of *M. Goeschon's* report on the discovery of the manuscript of Gaius, by the celebrated M. Niebuhr.

† For the Institutes of Gaius, and the Codes of Gregorian, and Hermogenes, see Brunquellus's Hist. Juris Romani, pp. 151, 152, 154.

Emperor Theodosius the Second. It is After Christ.
particularly remarkable for having furnished many new articles of great importance to the jurisprudence of Rome . 306

They chiefly arose from the foundation of Constantinople, the new forms of civil and military government introduced by Constantine, the legal establishment of Christianity, and the division of the empire between the sons of Theodosius the Great. To the first may be referred numerous laws, respecting the privileges and police of the imperial city; to the second, an abundance of legal provisions, respecting the various officers of the empire, and the ceremonial of the Byzantine court; to the third, a succession of imperial edicts, by which Christianity was first tolerated, then legalized, and afterwards became the established religion of the state.

The division of the empire between the sons of Theodosius, in 395, was attended with still more important effects on Roman jurisprudence 395

V. 7.

THE variety of laws, principally occasioned by the circumstances which have been mentioned, introduced a considerable degree of confusion into the Roman jurisprudence. To remedy it, Theodosius the Second, the Emperor of the East, published, in 438, the celebrated code of law, called from him the *Theodosian Code*, which forms THE SEVENTH PERIOD OF THE HISTORY OF THE ROMAN LAW. It comprises all the imperial constitutions, from 312, the year in which Constantine was supposed to have embraced Christianity, to the time of its publication. It has not reached us entire: an excellent edition of the remains of it was prepared by James Gothofred: it was after his decease, published at Lyons in 1665, in six volumes folio, generally bound in four. It is accompanied with Prolegomena, introductory chapters, a perpetual commentary and notes; the labour of thirty years; and no one, as Doctor Jortin

After Christ.

438

justly remarks, ever thought the time After Christ.
thrown away. No work perhaps can be mentioned, which contains more information on the antiquities of the early ages of the lower empire. In addition to the Theodosian Code, it comprises the subsequent novells of the Emperors Valentinian, Marcian, Majorian, Severus, and Anthemius.

Immediately after the publication of the Theodosian Code in the eastern empire, it was received into the empire of the west, by an edict of Valentinian the Third. In the east, it retained its force, till it was superseded by the Justinianean collection.

It retained, but indirectly, its authority longer in the west. The Barbarians, who invaded the empire, permitted the Romans to retain the use of their laws.
In 506, Alaric, king of the Visigoths in 506
Gaul, ordered a legal code to be prepared, in which the Roman and Gothic laws and usages should be formed into one body of law, for the general use of all his subjects; this was accordingly

done in the twenty-second year of his reign; and from Anianus, his Referendary, or Chancellor, by whom it was either compiled or published, it was called the *Breviarium Aniani.* It is an extract from the Gregorian, Hermogenian, and Theodosian Codes, the novells of the subsequent Emperors, the sentences of Paullus, the Institutes of Gaius, and the works of Papinian. It superseded the use of the former laws so far, that, in a short time, they ceased to be cited in the courts, or by writers on subjects of law; and Anianus's collection, under the name of the Roman or Theodosian law, became the only legal work of authority.* After Christ.

To this period also, must be ascribed the celebrated *Collatio Mosaicarum et Romanarum Legum:* the object of it is to shew the resemblance between the Mosaical institutions and the Roman law; the best edition of it is F. Desmare's in 1689.

* See the learned *Prolegomena ad Codicem Theodosianum* of Gothofred.

V. 8.

THE EIGHTH, AND MOST IMPORTANT, PERIOD, of the history of the Roman law, comprises the time in which the body of law, compiled by the direction of the Emperor Justinian, was framed. After Christ.

1. By his order, in the first year of his reign, Trebonian, and nine other persons of distinction, made a collection of the most useful laws, in the Codex Theodosianus, the two earlier codes of Gregorius and Hermogenes, and the constitutions of some succeeding emperors. It was immediately published by Justinian, and is called the *Codex Justinianeus Primæ Prælectionis* 528

2. But his great work is his *Digest or Pandects.* By his direction, Trebonian, with the assistance of sixteen persons, eminent either as magistrates or professors of law, extracted from the works of the former civilians, a complete system of law, and digested it into fifty books 533

3. Previously to its publication, an elementary treatise, comprising the general principles of the system of jurisprudence, contained in it, was promulgated, by the Emperor's direction, in four books. From its contents, it was called *The Institutes*. After Christ.

Thus the Digest and Institutes were formed into a body of law, by the authority of the Emperor. He addressed them, as imperial laws, to his tribunals of justice, and to all the academies, where the science of jurisprudence was taught: they were to supersede all other law, and to be the only legitimate system of jurisprudence throughout the empire.

4. In the following year, he published a corrected edition of the code, under the title *Codex Repetitæ Prelectionis*.— This wholly superseded the first code; and, except so far as the first code has been preserved in the latter, it is wholly lost 534

5. The edicts which he promulgated, after the new edition of the Codex, were collected into one volume, in the last

year of his reign, and published under the name of *Novellæ*. . . . . After Christ. 566

6. Most of the Novellæ were written in the Greek language. In the last year of Justinian's life, a Latin translation was made of them; and, by the fidelity with which it was executed, obtained the appellation of the *Volumen Authenticum*. 568

Other translations of the Novellæ have appeared: that, published at Marburgh, in 1717, by John Frederick Hemburgh, has the character of being extremely well executed, and is accompanied with a valuable commentary and notes.

7. In most editions of the Corpus Juris Civilis, the Novells are followed by the *Books of Fiefs, the Constitutions of Conrade the Third, and the Emperor Frederick*, under the title of *Decima Collatio*, and some other articles. But these make no part of what is called the Corpus Juris Civilis: that consists solely of the Pandects, the Institutes, the Codex Repetitæ Prælectionis, and the Novells.

8. On the *general merit of Justinian's*

Collection, as a body of written law, able judges have differed: the better opinion seems to be, that it is executed with great ability, but that it is open to much objection; the Responsa Prudentum sometimes being unfaithfully given in it; contradictory doctrines having found their way into it; the style of it being often too flowery; and its innovations on the old law, sometimes being injudicious. Heineccius, whose testimony, in this case, is of the greatest weight, at first judged of it unfavourably; but afterwards changed his opinion: he mentions, in high terms of commendation, the defence of it by Huberus and the Cocceii, and asserts that the cause must now be considered as decided in favour of Justinian. Hist. Juris Romani, Lib. I. § cccc.

The compilation of Justinian, as an attempt to reduce the size of the national law, wholly failed.

Taking into account the published decisions upon it, and the interpretations of it of acknowledged authority, the general bulk of the civil law probably exceeded, in every state of Europe governed by it, at the commencement of the French revolution, the size of the Roman law, when it was placed by Justinian in the hands of Tribonian.

In France, many successful attempts were made to simplify its law. With this view, several Ordonnances were promulgated. The *Ordonnance de Moulins* in the reign of Henry II. and the *Ordonnance sur la Marine*, framed under the direction of Colbert in the reign of Louis XIV. and those framed by the Chancellor d'Aguesseau in the following reign, have received universal approbation: those of D'Aguesseau are noticed in the preceding account of his life.

But to return to our subject. One circumstance may be mentioned, which seems to be an unquestionable proof that the Justinianean Collection possesses a very high degree of intrinsic merit. Notwithstanding the different forms of the governments of Europe, and the great variety of their political and judicial systems, the civil law has obtained either a general or a partial admittance into the jurisprudence of almost all of them: and, where it has been least favourably received, it has been pronounced a collection of written wisdom: this could not have happened, if it had not been deeply and extensively grounded on principles of justice and equity, applicable to the public and private concerns of mankind, at all times, and in every situation.

V. 9.

9. THE fate of this venerable body of law, promulgated with so much pomp, and possessing so much intrinsic merit, is singular, and forms THE NINTH PERIOD OF THE HISTORY OF THE ROMAN LAW.—The reign of the third successor of Justinian, was the last, in which it maintained its authority in the west. After that time, all law and regular government were rapidly destroyed by the Barbarians who invaded and overturned the Roman empire. The Exarchate of Ravenna, the last of their Italian victories, was conquered by them in 753; and that year is assigned as the æra of the final extinction of the Roman law in Italy 753

After Christ

It lingered longer in the east: in

strictness even, it cannot be said to have wholly lost its authority, in that part of the empire, till the taking of Constantinople, by Mahomet the Second. In the lifetime of Justinian, the Pandects were translated into Greek by Thallelæus; a translation of the Code was made, perhaps, by the same hand; and a Greek paraphrase of the Institutes was published by Theophilus. After Christ.

The successors of Justinian published different laws, some of which have reached us. In the reign of Basilius the Macedonian, and his sons Leo the philosopher, and Constantine Porphyrogenneta, an epitome, in sixty books, of Justinian's Code, and of the constitutions of succeeding emperors, was framed, under the title of *Basilica*. Forty- 906
one of the sixty books were splendidly published by Fabrot, at Paris, in 1647, in seven tomes in folio; four more have been published in Meerman's Thesaurus.

That the Basilica superseded, in the eastern empire, the immediate authority of the Justinianean collection, is true;

but, that the Justinianean collection After Christ.
formed a considerable part, and was, in fact, the groundwork of the Basilica, is unquestionable. Thus, through the medium of the Basilica, the code of Justinian, in a great degree, directed or influenced the jurisprudence of the eastern empire, to the latest moment of its existence.* 1453

V. 10.

THE text of the Pandects being almost wholly lost, accident led, sometime about the year 1137, to the discovery of a complete copy of them, at Almaphi, a town in Italy, near Salerno. This forms the TENTH PERIOD OF THE HISTORY OF THE ROMAN LAW. From Amalphi the copy found its way to Pisa; and Pisa having submitted to the Florentines, in 1406, the copy was removed in great triumph
to Florence. By the direction of the 1406
magistrates of the town, it was imme-

* See Appendix, Note III.

diately bound, in a superb manner, and deposited in a costly chest. This copy of it is generally called the Florentine Pandects. Formerly they were shewn only by torch-light, in the presence of two magistrates, and two Cistercian monks, with their heads uncovered. They have been successively collated by Politian, Bolognini, and Antonius Augustinus; an exact copy of them was published in 1553, by Franciscus Taurellus; for its accuracy and beauty, this edition ranks high among the ornaments of the press: it should be accompanied, with the treatise of Antonius Augustinus, on the proper names in the Pandects, published by him at Tarragona, in 1579. About the year 1710, Henry Brencman, a Dutchman, was permitted, at the earnest solicitation of our George the First, to collate the manuscript. He employed ten years upon it, and in the investigation of various topics of literature connected with the Justinianean Code. His elegant and curious *Historia Pandectarum*, published at Utrecht, in 1722, gives an interesting account of his labours; and shews, like the labours of Wetstein and Mill, that great fire of imagination, exquisite taste, minute and patient investigation, and the soundest judgment, may be found in the same mind.—Some have supposed that the Florentine manuscript, is the autograph of the Pandects; for this opinion there is no real ground or authority; but Brencman refers it to the sixth century, a period not very remote from the æra of Justinian. Brencman's work forms a small part of an original design, and is so ably executed that all must lament his having left any part of his design unfinished.—See *Georgii Christiani Gebaveri Narratio de Henrico Brencmanno, et de Manuscriptis Brencmannianis, Gottingæ* 1764. The possession of Brencman's Manuscripts would be a valuable acquisition to a Public Library.

Three editions of the Pandects are particularly distinguished,—the Norican Edition published by Holoander, at Nuremberg, in 1529, in three volumes quarto: the Florentine, published by Taurellus, at Florence, in 1553, in two volumes folio, often bound in three; and the Vulgate, under which name some understand every edition which is not taken from the Norican or Florentine edition; others, an edition in common use, before the publication of those editions: but this edition it would be difficult, perhaps impossible, to point out. The best editions for general use appear to be Pothier's Pandectæ Justinianeæ, published at Lyons in 1782, in three volumes folio; and that of Dionysius Gothofred, published by Simon Van Leeuwen at Leyden in 1663, in one large volume, generally bound in two:—It contains the Institutes, the Digest, the Code, the Fasti Consulares, Freher's Chronologia Imperii Utriusque, Gothofred's Epitome of the Novells of Justinian, various other edicts and novell constitutions, Frederici II. Imp. Extravagantes, Liber de Pace Constantiæ, Gothofred's Epitome of the books of the Fiefs, an extensive synopsis of Civil Law, the fragments of the Twelve Tables, the Tituli of Ulpian, and the opinions of Paulus, with notes, and copious indexes to the whole.*

* This article is extracted—from *Pomponius's short treatise de Origine Juris et omnium magistratuum et successione prudentum, Dig. tit.* 2; *the Preface to the Institutes*; *the first, second, and third Prefaces to the Pandects*; *the first and second Prefaces to the Code*; *Heineccius's Historia Juris Civilis Romani ac Germanici, Lugd. Bat.* 1740, *8vo.*; *the Antiquitatum Romanarum Syntagma, of the same*

VI.

WE are now led to an inquiry respecting THE PRINCIPAL SCHOOLS, IN WHICH THE CIVIL LAW HAS BEEN TAUGHT since its revival in Europe.

author, Strasburgh 1724, *8vo.*—The writings of Heineccius are a striking proof of the truth of Mr. Gibbon's observation, (vol. 4. 395, note 160), " that the universities of Holland and Branden-" burgh, in the beginning of the last century, " appear to have studied the civil law on the most " just and liberal principles:"—From *the works of Gravina, on the Civil Law, Leipsiæ* 1717, *in three volumes* 4*to, particularly his Origines Juris Civilis:* Gravina's account of the *Leges* and *Senatus Consulta* is particularly interesting:—From *Brunquellus's Historia Juris Romano-Germanici, Amst.* 1730, *8vo.* perhaps the completest historical account extant of the Roman law; *Struvius's Historia Juris Romani, Jenæ* 1718, 4*to.*; *Pothier's Prolegomena* to his *Pandectæ Justinianeæ, Lyons,* 3 *vols. fol.*; *Terasson's Histoire de la Jurisprudence Romaine, Paris* 1750, said by Mr. Gibbon, (4th vol. note 9), to be " a work of more promise than performance;" *Thomasius's Delineatio Historiæ Juris Romani et Germanici, Erfordiæ* 1750, *8vo. and his Nævorum Jurisprudentiæ Romanæ Libri duo, Halæ Magdæburgicæ* 1707, *8vo.*—they contain a severe attack on the Justinianean collection, on the

In the early days of the republic, it was usual for such as desired to gain a knowledge of the laws of their country, to attend on those who were consulted on legal subjects, at the hours, in which these consultations generally took place. Tiberius Coruncanius is said, by

emperor, and all other persons concerned in it:—From *Montesquieu's Esprit des Loix*, a work entitled to all the praise it has received; no one, who has not travelled much through the Corpus Juris and the Capitularies, can form an idea of the comprehensive brevity and energy of this work of Montesquieu. The writer invites every student, who has bewildered himself among the *Cognati* and *Agnati* of the Roman law, to peruse the 27th Book *de l'Esprit des Loix*, where he will find the whole system of Roman jurisprudence respecting heirship and succession fully developed, with the greatest precision and perspicuity; it consists of a single chapter; but it is a chapter written by one, who, as he himself says of Tacitus, "*abrégeoit tout, parce* "*qu'il voyait tout:*"—From *Dr. Bever's History of the Legal Polity of the Roman State, Lond.* 1781, 4*to.*; *Dr. Taylor's Elements of the Civil Law, Camb.* 1755, 4*to.* a work, if we acquiesce in Mr. Gibbon's opinion of it, (4th vol. note 132), "of amusing, though various reading; but which "cannot be praised for philosophical precision:"—From *the four Books of Justinian, translated by the late Dr. Harris, with notes and a preface*; the translation is excellent, and it is much to be

Cicero, to have been the first among the Romans, who professed to give regular instructions on legal subjects. Afterwards, public schools of jurisprudence were established; the most celebrated were those at Rome and Constantinople; Justinian founded a third at Berytus, and used all means in his power, to promote its success: he gave the professors large salaries, and advanced some of them to offices of high distinction in the state;—as the authority of his law decreased, they fell into decay.

With the discovery of the Pandects at Amalphi, the study of the civil law revived:—it was introduced into several universities, and exercises were performed, lectures read, and degrees conferred in this, as in other branches

lamented, that the preface is not longer, and the notes more copious:—From *Ferriere's Histoire du Droit Romaine, Paris* 1783, *8vo.*; *Beaufort's Republique Romaine, Paris* 1767, 6 *vols.* *8vo.* an excellent constitutional History of the Roman Government:—From *the* 44*th Chapter of the* 4*th Volume of Mr. Gibbon's History*; *M. Bouchaud's Recherches Historiques sur les Edits des Magistrats Romains, Quatrième Memoire, Mem. de l'Academie,* 41*st vol. p.* 1:—and from *Mr. Schomberg's Elements of Roman Law, London* 1786, *8vo.*

of science, and several nations of the continent adopted it, as the basis of their several constitutions. From this time, there has been a regular succession of civil lawyers, distinguished by some circumstance or other into different classes, or as it is usually expressed, into different schools.

1. The first, is *the school of Irnerius*, a learned German, who had acquired his knowledge of the civil law, at Constantinople. He taught it at Bologna, with great applause: the legal schism which had divided the Sabinians and Proculeians, was revived, in some degree, among his scholars: one of them, was the celebrated Azo, a Proculeian, whose writings, Montesquieu is said to have preferred to all other on the subject of civil law. A more important subject, the contest between the emperors and popes, produced a more serious warfare between the disciples of Irnerius. The German emperors, who pretended to succeed to the empire of the Cæsars, claimed the same extent of empire in the west, and with the same privileges, as it had been held by the Cæsars; to this claim, the spirit and language of the civil law being highly

favourable, the emperors encouraged the civilians; and, in return for it, had their pens at command. The popes were supported by the canonists; and the canonists found, in the decree of Gratian, as much to favour the pretensions of the popes, as the civilians found, in the law of Justinian, to favour the pretensions of the emperors. Thus, generally speaking, the civilians were Ghibelins, the name given to the partisans of the emperors, and the canonists were Guelphs, the name given to the partisans of the popes. But this distinction did not prevail so far, as to prevent many canonists from being Ghibelins, or many civilians from being Guelphs; those among the civilians, who sided with the canonists in these disputes, were called from the decree of Gratian, *Decretistæ*, in opposition to the rest of the body, who assumed the appellation of *Legistæ*, from their adherence to the supposed Ghibelin doctrines of the civil law.

2. *A new school began with Accursius:*— his Gloss is a perpetual commentary on the text of Justinian: it was once considered as legal authority, and was therefore usually published with the text:—it is even now

respected as an useful commentary. Accursius had many disciples, whose glosses had great celebrity in their day, but are now wholly forgotten.

3. *Bartolus, and Baldus his disciple and rival, gave rise to a new school,* famous for copious commentaries on Justinian's text; for the idle subtleties with which they abound, and for their barbarous style.

4. Andrew Alciat was the first who united the study of polite learning and antiquity, with the study of the civil law: he was the founder of a *new school, which is called the Cujacian* from Cujas, the glory of civilians. Of Cujas, it may be said truly, that he found the civil law of wood, and left it of marble. That school has subsisted to the present time; it has never been without writers of the greatest taste, judgment and erudition; the names of Cujacius, Augustinus, the Gothofredi, Heineccius, Voetius, Gravina, and Pothier, are as dear to the scholar, as they are to the lawyer. An Englishman, however, must reflect with pleasure, that his countryman, Mr. Justice Blackstone's Commentaries on the Laws of England, will not suffer in a comparison with

any foreign work of jurisprudence;—perhaps it will be difficult to name one of the same nature, which will bear a comparison with it.*

VII.

It remains to give some account of THE INFLUENCE OF THE CIVIL LAW ON THE JURISPRUDENCE OF THE MODERN STATES OF EUROPE.

On the degree of its influence on the law of Germany, the German lawyers are not agreed: but it is a mere dispute of words; all of them allow that more causes are decided in their courts, by the rules of the civil law, than by the laws of Germany; and that, where the laws of Germany do not interfere, the subject in dispute must be tried by the civil law; after these concessions, it is not material to inquire, whether, to use the language of the German lawyers, the civil law be the dominant law of Germany, or subsidiary to it.

The same may be said of its influence in Bohemia, Hungary, Poland, and Scotland.

* This article is chiefly taken from the cited works of *Gravina* and *Brunquellus*.

At Rome, and in all the territories of the pope, it is received without limitation; in most other parts of Italy, including Naples and the two Sicilies, it has nearly the same influence; except where the feudal policy intervenes.

It's influence in Spain and Portugal is more qualified; but it appears to be admitted, that where the law of the country does not provide the contrary, the civil law shall decide: and it is the settled practice, that no person shall be appointed a judge or received an advocate in any of the courts of law, who has not been a student in some academy of civil or canon law for ten years.

The provinces of France, which lie nearest to Italy, were the first conquered by the Romans, and the last conquered by the Francs. At the time of the conquest of them by the Francs, they were wholly governed by the Roman law: they are the provinces of Guyenne, Provençe, Dauphiné, and, speaking generally, all the provinces, under the jurisdiction of Toulouse, Bourdeaux, Grenoble, Aix, and Pau; the Lyonnois, Forez, Beaujolois, and a great part of Auvergne. Their

Francic conquerors permitted them to retain the Roman law; where it has not been altered, they are still governed by it: and, from this circumstance, they are known under the general name of the Pays du Droit Ecrit. The remaining part of France is governed by the different laws and customs of the provinces of which it is composed, and from this circumstance, is called, Pays Coutumier.

The Venetians have always disclaimed the authority of the civil law.

It was introduced into England by Theobald, a Norman Abbot, who was elected to the see of Canterbury. He placed Roger, surnamed Vacarius, in the university of Oxford:—students flocked to him in such abundance, as to excite the jealousy of government, and the study of the civil law was prohibited by King Stephen. It continued, however, to be encouraged by the clergy, and became so favourite a pursuit, that almost all, who aspired to the high offices of church or state, thought it necessary to go through a regular course of civil law, to qualify themselves for them:—it became a matter of reproach to the clergy, that they quitted the canon for the civil law;

and pope Innocent prohibited the very reading of it by them. Notwithstanding this opposition, the study of the civil law has been encouraged in this country:—in each of our universities there is a professor of civil law, and, by general custom and immemorial usage, some of the institutions of the civil law have been received into our national law. In the spiritual courts, in the courts of both the universities, the military courts, and courts of admiralty, the rules of civil law, and its form of legal proceeding greatly prevail. But the courts of common law have a superintendency over these courts, and from all of them, an appeal lies to the King in the last resort. "From these strong marks and ensigns of "superintendency it appears beyond doubt," says Mr. Justice Blackstone, "that the civil "and canon laws, though admitted in some "cases by custom, and in some courts, are "only subordinate and leges sub graviore "lege."—The short but very learned treatise of Arthur Duck, *de Usu et Auctoritate juris civilis in Dominiis principum christianorum*, conveys, in elegant language and a pleasing manner, complete information on the nature and extent of the influence of the civil law, on the jurisprudence of the modern states of Europe.

HISTORICAL AND LITERARY ACCOUNT

OF

THE CANON LAW.

THE following pages, after some introductory matter respecting, I. the religious worship and hierarchy of Pagan Rome; II. respecting the rise and progress of Christianity, from its being the most persecuted sect, till its becoming the established church of the Roman empire; and III. respecting the principal orders of the Christian hierarchy;—will contain, IV. a mention of the general materials, and V. an historical account of the particular documents, of which the CANON Law is composed.

I.

I. 1. It seems generally understood that the ANTIENT RELIGION OF ROME was of Celtic extraction, without images, without temples, and with few religious rites; that Numa established many ceremonies, and built a temple for sacrifices to the one eternal God; that, in other respects, he left the religion of Rome in its original simplicity; and that Tarquinius Priscus introduced into it the superstitions of the Greeks and Hetruscans.

I. 2. THE GODS, whom the Romans worshipped, were divided into the *Dii Majorum Gentium*, or the great cœlestial deities, with the *Dii Selecti*, and the *Dii Minorum Gentium*, or the inferior gods. The cœlestial deities were twelve in number: Jupiter, the king of gods and men; Juno, his sister and wife; Minerva, the goddess of wisdom; Vesta, the goddess of fire; Ceres, the goddess of corn and husbandry; Neptune, the god of the sea; Venus, the goddess of love and beauty; Vulcan, the god of fire; Mars, the god of war; Mercury, the god of eloquence and trade; Apollo, the god of music, poetry, medicine and augury; and Diana, the goddess of the woods. The *Dii Selecti* were Saturn, the god of time; Janus, the god of the year, and Rhea his wife; Pluto, the king of the infernal regions; Bacchus, the god of wine; Sol, the sun; Luna, the moon; and Genius, each man and each place's tutelary god. The *Dii Minorum Gen-*

tium were the *Dii Indigetes*, or heroes ranked among the gods on account of their heroic virtues, as Hercules, Castor and Pollux, Æneas and Romulus; the *Dii Semones*, or *Semihomines*, less than gods, and greater than men, as Pan, Pomona, Flora, Terminus, the Nymphs.

I. 3. To the service of these gods, *several colleges of priests* were dedicated:—*Fifteen Pontiffs*, whose office it was to judge and determine on all sacred things; fifteen Augurs, who, from the flight, chirping or feeding of birds, and fifteen Aruspices, who, from the entrails of victims derived omens of futurity, the Quindecemviri, who had the care of the Sibylline books; the Septemviri, who prepared the sacred feasts; the Fratres Ambarvales, who offered up sacrifices for the fertility of the grounds; the Curiones, who officiated in the Curiæ; the Feciales, or sacred persons employed in declaring war and making peace; the Sodales Titii, whose office it was to preserve the sacred rites of the Sabines; and *the Rex Sacrorum*, to whom that title was given from his performing certain sacred rites, which could only be performed by royal hands.

In addition to these, each god had his Flamines, or particular priests. The six vestal virgins had the care of the sacred fire in the temple of Vesta, and the secret pledges of the eternal duration of Rome were intrusted to them. Every part of the empire abounded with temples and statues, and in every temple and statue a divine something was supposed to reside.

When we consider the general absurdity of the pagan creed, we find it difficult to suppose, that any rational mind could seriously believe its doctrines, or that it should become the national religion of a great and sensible people. Those doubts increase on us, when we see how often the religious prejudices of the Romans were used by the leading men of Rome, as an engine for political purposes; when we consider the ridicule with which the less and even the greater deities were treated by their poets, philosophers, and historians; and when we read the passages in the works of Cicero and other writers, in which, often indirectly, and sometimes in the most direct terms, they deliver it as their opinion, that, in religion there are many truths, which it is not expedient the vulgar should know; and many falsehoods, which it is useful for the people to receive as truths. But there is reason to believe, that till the Greek philosophy found its way into Rome, the general body of the Romans was sincere in the worship of their gods; and that, even after the introduction of the Greek philosophy, the number of those who gave up the whole of the national creed was very small. A freedom, even from the lowest kind of superstition, is often mentioned by their writers as a great effort of the human mind: and the writings of Cicero demonstratively prove, that those who rejected the popular superstition, had no settled system of religious belief to substitute in its place. The total extirpation of pagan superstition, which pagan philosophy could not effect, it is the triumph of Christianity to have accomplished; and to have introduced at the same time, a simple and sublime religion, accommodated to all persons, all times, all nations, and all circumstances; on which the weak and the strong may equally rely.*

* Beaufort, Rep. Rom. l. 1. Adams's Roman Antiquities, 281—303.

II.

By the law of Athens, the act of introducing foreign deities was punished with death. The law of Rome was not so severe: Mosheim and Bynkershoek seem to prove, that though the Romans would not allow any change to be made in the religions which were publicly professed in the empire, nor any new form of worship to be openly introduced, yet that, except when it threatened danger to the state, they granted a FREE TOLERATION OF FOREIGN WORSHIP, not only to individuals, but to bodies of men.

The Christians, whose mild, unassuming, and benevolent morality entitled them to universal good will, were alone denied the benefit of this general toleration. From the reign of Nero, till the triumph of Constantine the Great over his rival Licinius, they were always treated with harshness, and repeatedly suffered the severest persecutions.

The favour of Constantine to them was, immediately after his first successes, shewn by his repeal of the laws enacted against them. By the edict of Milan, he restored them to all their civil and religious rights, and allowed them, in common with the rest of his subjects, the free choice and exercise of their religion. In the general dispensation of his favours, he held, with an impartial hand, the balance between his christian and heathen subjects. His successors, except during the short interval of Julian's reign, strongly encouraged christianity and discountenanced heathenism; and finally, by the edicts of Theodosius, the antient worship of Rome was proscribed, and christianity became the established religion of the empire. Till those edicts, the spirit of polytheism, had lingered among the principal nobility of Rome; after them, it lingered among the Grecian philosophers: but by his edict in 529, Justinian silenced the schools of Athens; and to that æra, the final extinction of Paganism is always assigned.*

* *Francis Balduinus, Commentarius ad edicta Imperatorum in Christianos, Edit. Gudling; Bynkershoek, Dissertatio de Cultu Peregrinæ Religionis apud Romanos, in Opusculis, Lugd. Bat.* 1719; *Mosheim, de Rebus Christianorum ante Constantinum Magnum Commentarii, Helmstadii,* 4*to.* 1753, *c.* 1. *sect.* 8; *Seculum primum,* 27—32. In his *Six Letters on Intolerance, London,* 1791, *Sir Geo.*

III.

In respect to the CHRISTIAN HIERARCHY, the Roman empire, at the time when Christianity obtained in it a legal establishment, under Constantine the Great, had reached its utmost limits. It was divided into four Præfectures:—the Eastern, which comprised the country between Thrace and Persia, the Caucasus and the Cataracts of the Nile; the Præfecture of Illyricum, which comprised Pannonia, Dacia, Macedonia, and Greece; the Præfecture of Italy, which comprised Italy, Rhœtia, the Islands of the Mediterranean, and the part of Africa from the westernmost mouth of the Nile to Tingitana; and the Præfecture of the Gauls, which comprised Spain, Britain, and the part of Africa from Tingitana to the western ocean. Each præfecture was divided into several dioceses; each diocese into several provinces; and in each province there was one, and sometimes

Colebrooke has collected many curious facts, to shew that the religious toleration of the Romans was by no means so perfect as is generally thought.

more than one mother-town, on which other towns depended. The dioceses were thirteen in number, the provinces one hundred and twenty.

In the establishment of her hierarchy, the Christian church, particularly in the east, appears to have conformed very much to this model. Before the translation of the seat of the Roman empire to Constantinople, the church had the three Patriarchates of Rome, Antioch, and Alexandria; after its translation, the bishops of Constantinople acquired importance; by degrees they obtained ecclesiastical jurisdiction over Thrace, Asia, and Pontus, and were elevated to the rank of patriarch: afterwards, the same rank was conferred on the bishop of Jerusalem: and, according to Mr. Gibbon's observation, (vol. vi. p. 378), the Roman bishop was always respected as the first of the five patriarchs. Thus, speaking generally, the patriarchs corresponded in rank with the prefects; in each diocese there was a primate; in each province, one or more than one metropolitan; and each metropolitan had under him a certain number of suffragan bishops. Regular funds, proportioned to their respective ranks, were appropriated for their support; except in cases of singular enormity they were exempted from the civil jurisdiction of the magistrate; and, in many other important articles a distinction between the clergy and the laity, wholly unknown in the law of heathen Rome, was admitted into the Codes of the Christian emperors.*

IV.

THE liberty of holding ecclesiastical assemblies was one of the most important privileges of the dignified members of the clergy. Occasional assemblies were convened of all the bishops in the Christian world, or of all the bishops within the limits of a patriarchate: and, generally in the spring and autumn of

* *Frederici Spanhemii, Geographia Sacra, Distributio Diœceseon et Provinciarum, inde a Temporibus Constantini Magni in orbe utroque, orientali et occidentali*; *inter Opera Omnia, Lugduni Batavorum, fol.* 1 *vol.* 75—204; *Bingham's Antiquities of the Christian Church, London* 1726, *fol.* 2 *vol. lib.* 9; *Du Pin, de Antiquâ Ecclesiæ Disciplina, Par.* 1686; *Petrus de la Marca, Concordia Sacerdotii atque Imperii, fol. Paris* 1704.

every year, the metropolitan convened the bishops of his province to debate on its religious concerns. From Concilium, which, among the Romans, denoted a select meeting, in contradistinction to Comitia, which they used to denote general meetings, these assemblies received, in the Latin church, the appellation of councils; in the Greek church, they were called synods; at a subsequent time, the word council still retaining its original import, the word synod was used, in the Latin church, to denote the assembly of a bishop and his clergy. The Scripture is the first, the decrees of the councils are the second source, from which THE MATERIALS OF THE CANON LAW are drawn. The decrees and decretals of the popes are the third; the works of the fathers and other respectable writers are the fourth. By the decrees of the popes are meant their decrees in the councils held by them in Italy; the decretals are their answers to questions proposed to them on religious subjects.

V.

Those, who profess to give an HISTORICAL ACCOUNT OF THE CANON LAW, divide it into three periods: the Antient, the Middle, and the Modern:—the antient, begins with the first, and ends with the eighth century, when Isidore Mercator's collection of canons made its appearance; the middle, begins with that century, and ends with the council of Pisa, in 1409; the modern, begins with that council, and extends to the present time.

V. 1.

The ANTIENT PART OF THE HISTORY OF THE CANON LAW is remarkable for several Collections of Canons.

1. Some are *CANONS OF THE GENERAL CHURCH.*

The first collection of these canons is called the *Apostolic Canons.* They have been ascribed to the apostles; it has been said, that St. Clement, the immediate successor of St. Peter, was the collector of them. If the apostles had really promulgated them, it is difficult to assign a reason for their not having been admitted to a place in the writings which form the New Testament; but, of the antient fathers, St. John Damascene alone has done them that honour. From their being omitted in the canon of the New Testament, from the universal silence of the fathers of the three first ages respecting them, from the mention in them of many offices and customs, which there is every reason to suppose of a later origin, from no appeals having been made to them in the controversies which arose in times subsequent to them, and on which their language is decisive, and from no mention having been made of them in the synod held at Rome in 496, which mentions all the writings of the Old and New Testament, they are now considered to have been fabricated. Bishop Beveridge, who has published them with learned notes, supposes they were framed under the sanction of bishops, who held the sees founded by the apostles, and that they were collected towards the end of the second or beginning of the third century. The first regular mention of them is found in the second council of Constantinople. After Christ.

The Greek church, at least since the synod in Trullo, in 692, has singularly respected them, and considered the 85 first of them as authentic: the Latin church seems to have admitted the 50 first of them. They were first printed at Venice in 1563, in 4to, and have often been reprinted 200

The Apostolic Constitutions are of high antiquity, have been much interpolated, and are of no authority. It is supposed that they first appeared in the fourth century 300

2. Hitherto, the canons spoken of are the canons of the general church: there also are *CANONS OF PARTICULAR CHURCHES.*

In respect to the *Greek Church,* the first collection of canons which has come down to us from the Greek church, is the *Codex Ecclesiæ Orientalis.* It is supposed to have been first published in . 385

This collection contains 165 canons:

20 of them are canons of the general council of Nice; 24, are canons of the council of Ancyra; 14, are of the council of Neocesarea; 20, of the council of Gangris; 25, of the council of Antioch; 59, of the council of Laodicea; and three of the first council of Constantinople. The council of Chalcedon mentions this collection with approbation. After Christ.

The second collection of canons of the Greek church is, the *Codex Ecclesiæ Universæ* 451

It comprises the canons in the preceding collection, with the addition of some omitted canons of the council of Constantinople, some of the council of Ephesus, and some of the council of Chalcedon.

Both these collections are confined to the canons of the councils of the oriental churches; but they by no means include all the canons of all the councils of those churches.

About the middle of the sixth century, John, then a priest of Antioch, afterwards patriarch of Constantinople, published a collection of the Greek canons, digested under fifty heads, according to the subjects of them. He afterwards published an abridgment of it: the first is called his *Collection of Canons*; the second his *Nomo-Canon:* he is generally called Joannes Scholasticus 560

After Christ.

We know little more of the canons of the Greek church till the *Synod in Trullo*. By that synod, a code was formed of the canons framed at it, of those framed at the synods of Carthage, and at the council of Constantinople, held by Nectarius, and of some writings of the Fathers. To those were added the twenty-two canons of the second council of Nice, and the fourth council of Constantinople 692

Here, before the schism, which separated the Greek from the Latin church, the code of the Greek canon law rested. Under Photius, two councils were held at Constantinople: the canons of those councils were received by the schismatic churches of the east, and were published by Photius in his *Nomo-Canon*, or modern collection of canons, in 883

With the *Commentaries of Balsamon, Zonaras, and Aristenus*, and other curious articles, and with a learned preface, all these collections of canons were published, at Oxford, by Dr. Beveridge, afterwards Bishop of St. Asaph, under the title, "*Pandectæ* "*Canonum Sanctorum Apostolorum et Conci-* "*liorum ab Ecclesiâ Græca receptorum.*" "Those," says Van Espen, "who will read with "attention, the notes of the learned editor, "will find much very learned exposition of the "canon law, and much instructive matter on "other subjects, connected with the learn- "ing of the canons." "Bishop Beveridge's "works," says L'Advocat, professor of Theology in the Sorbonne, "are written with so "much dignity, majesty, learning, and mo- "desty, that he is thought, with reason, to be "one of the greatest and most learned men "whom England has produced." An epistolary correspondence was carried on between him and Bossuet.

3. In the *LATIN CHURCH*, frequent mention is made of the *Vetus Canonum Latinorum Editio*. It was superseded by the collection made by *Dionysius Exiguus*,

about the beginning of the sixth century. That collection was afterwards enlarged by the decrees of Pope Symmachus, Pope Hormisdas, and Pope Gregory the Second. This collection was of great authority both in the Greek and the Latin churches.

4. Other Churches had their Collections of Canons. The *CHURCH OF AFRICA* had hers: the *Breviatio Canonum of Fulgentius Ferrandus*, and the *Breviarium* and *Concordia Canonum of Cresconius*, are added to it.

The *CHURCH OF SPAIN* also had her collection of canons. It is attributed to St. Isidore, Bishop of Seville; from his diocese, he is frequently distinguished by the appellation of Hispalensis.

In 790, Pope Adrian presented Charlemagne with a collection of canons. It was composed of the collection of Dionysius Exiguus, and the epistles of several popes.

At the council held at Canterbury in 873, a book of canons was produced, and approved of; but we do not know what canons it contained.

V. 2.

1. The MIDDLE PERIOD OF THE HISTORY OF THE CANON LAW commences with the ninth century, at the beginning of which, or towards the end of the preceding century, *the collection of Isidore Peccator or Mercator* probably made its appearance . . . 760

After Christ.

It was brought from Spain into Germany by Riculphus, the bishop of Mayence. Who the compiler of it was, and why he assumed the name of Peccator or Mercator, are merely matters of conjecture. It sets out with describing the manner in which a council should be held; then the fifty first of the canons of the apostles follow: "Deinde," says the author, "quarumdam epistolarum "decreta virorum apostolicorum inse- "ruimus, id est, Clementis, Anacleti, "Evaristi, et cæterorum apostolicorum, "quas potuimus hactenus reperire, epis- "tolas usque ad Sylvestrem Papam."

These are the celebrated decretals, concerning which, since the beginning

of the sixteenth century, there has been After Christ.
so much dispute among the learned. They seem to have made their first appearance in Germany: afterwards, to have been received in France, and, by degrees, in every part of the western church. For seven centuries after their first appearance, neither their authenticity nor their authority appears to have been questioned.

They were first attacked by Marsilius of Padua, then, by Cardinal Nicholas of Cusa, during the Council of Basil, and afterwards by Erasmus. In the celebrated Centuriators of Magdeburgh, in Blondel, and, lastly, in Van Espen, they have met with most powerful adversaries: in the author of the celebrated treatise, "*Quis est Petrus*," they have found both a zealous and an able advocate: but he seems to concede, that so much spuriousness is proved on them as to make them, when they stand alone, of no authority.

They were followed by what are
called the *Capitularies of Adrian* . . 845

The tenth century was famous for the *Collection of Rheginon, Abbot of Prumia* . . . . 906 (After Christ.)

The eleventh, for the collection of Burchardus, bishop of Wormes, entitled *Magnum Decretorum seu Canonum Volumen* 1000

The twelfth, for the collection of St. Ivo, the good lawyer. Two works are attributed to him: the *Decretum Canonum*, certainly belongs to him; his right to the second, the *Panomia*, is uncertain 1100

2. We now come to the celebrated *Decretum Gratiani*, or the *Concordia Discordantium Canonum*. Gratian was a Benedictine monk, in a monastery of Bologna. His work is an epitome of Canon Law, drawn from the decrees of councils, the letters of pontiffs, and the writings of antient doctors. Pope Eugenius the third was extremely satisfied with the work: and it was soon adopted in every part of the western church 1150

It is divided into three parts: the

first contains 101 distinctions or heads, and treats of the origin and different kinds of law, and particularly of the sources of ecclesiastical law, of persons in holy orders, and the hierarchy. The second contains thirty-six causes, as they are called, or particular cases, on which questions of difficulty arise: the third is divided into five distinctions, and contains a collection of canons relating to the consecration of churches, the sacraments, and the celebration of the divine office. The whole contains about 3000 canons or capitularies. Some are intitled *Paleæ*, the meaning of which word is not yet ascertained by the learned. After Christ.

This celebrated collection abounds with errors. Towards the middle of the sixteenth century, Antonius Demochares and Antonius Contius, the former a divine, the latter a canonist, published a corrected edition of it.

A more correct edition of it we owe to the council of Trent. By a decree of that council, it was ordered that

correct editions of missals, breviaries, After Christ.
and other books relating to ecclesiastical matters, should be published.

In consequence of this decree, pope Pius the fourth engaged several learned men in the correction of the decree of Gratian. The work was continued through the Pontificate of Pius the fifth. Gregory the thirteenth, the immediate successor of Pius the fifth, when a cardinal, had been employed on the work: under his auspices, it was finally published about the year . . 1580

Several faulty passages still remain in it. Many of them have been pointed out by Antonius Augustinus, the Archbishop of Tarragon, in his learned and entertaining dialogues on the *Emendation of Gratian.*

Such is the celebrated decree of Gratian, which for 800 years, has, in every country in Christendom, been considered a valuable repository of Canon Law.—To the compilations of Isidore and Gratian, one of the greatest misfortunes of the church, the claim of the popes to temporal power by divine right, may in some measure be attributed. That a claim so unfounded and so impious, so detrimental to religion, and so hostile to the peace of the world, should have been made, is strange—stranger yet, is the success it met with. After Christ.

It was soon observed, that the author had omitted in his collection several important articles. This gave rise to subsequent collections. The principal are the *Breviarium of Bernardus Papiensis*, and the *Collections of Johannes Galensis* and *Peter Beneventanus*. Of these, the last only was formally approved by the see of Rome. Pope Innocent the third published a collection of his own decretal epistles. His example was followed by Honorius the third, his immediate successor.

From these five collections, and from some decretals of his own, pope Gregory the ninth commissioned St. Raymond of Pennafort, a Dominican, to form a new collection of canons. He executed the work greatly to the satisfaction of his holiness; and, under his auspices, it was published about the year 1230, under the title *Libri quinque Decretalium Gregorii Noni.* It contains all the decrees of the council of Lateran, and the decisions of many popes on particular cases. It is divided into five books 1230

After Christ.

A further addition to the code of Canon Law was made by Pope Boniface the eighth. It contains the decretals of all the popes, subsequent to Gregory the ninth, and the decretals of that pope. It is called *Liber Sextus Decretalium,* and was published in 1298

On account of the differences between pope Boniface and Philip the Fair, it was not received in France.

The Liber Sextus Decretalium is followed by the collection, called sometimes *Liber Septimus Decretalium,* and sometimes *Clementis Papæ Constitutiones.* It was framed by pope Clement the fifth; and consists of his own decretals, particularly the canons of the council of Vienne, at which he presided. He promulgated it in 1313

The last article in the code of Canon Law is the *Extravagantes*. At first, every collection of Canon Law, except the decree of Gratian, was ranked among the Extravagantes. In the course of time, that name remained only to the collection of which we are now speaking. It is divided into two articles, the *Extravagantes Joannis XXII.* or the decretals of that pope, published by him about the year . . . . . . 1340 — After Christ.

And the *Extravagantes Communes*, consisting of the decrees of popes from Urban the sixth to Sixtus the fourth. It was published about the year . . . 1483

Neither of them is considered to be of authority. The first (published under the name of pope John the twenty-second,) was never formally approved of or sanctioned by him, and the author of the latter collection is wholly unknown.

A collection by Peter Matthæi was published in 1590

In some modern editions of the Corpus Juris Canonici, it is inserted under the title of the *Liber Septimus Decretalium*.

With these, what is called the Corpus Juris Canonici and the middle period of the history of the Canon Law closes. After Christ.

But mention should also be made of the *Institutiones Juris Canonici*, a compendium of Canon Law, published by Lancellot, a lawyer of Perugium, in 1563. By the direction of pope Pius the fifth, but without any confirmation of it by him, it was subjoined to the Corpus Juris Canonici, and has been published with it. "The Roman pontiffs," says Arthur Duck, (de Auctoritate Juris Civilis, lib. 1. c. 6. tit. 8.) "effected that, in the church, which "Justinian effected in the Roman em-"pire: they caused Gratian's decree to "be published in imitation of the Pan-"dects; the Decretals in imitation of "the Code; the Clementinæ and Ex-"travagantes, in imitation of the No-"vells; and to perfect the work, Paul "the fourth ordered Lancellot to com-"pose the Institutes; and under Gre-"gory the thirteenth, they were pub-

" lished at Rome, and added to the " Corpus Juris Canonici." In the edition of the Institutions of Lancellot, published in 1584, and in several subsequent editions, it is accompanied with a perpetual gloss, and followed by a commentary, written by Lancellot, which gives an account of the rise and progress of the work; and by a comparison of the Civil and Canon Law, also written by him 1563

V. 3.

THE MODERN PERIOD OF THE CANON LAW begins with the Council of Pisa, and extends to the present time.

The principal articles of canonical learning which have appeared during this period, are,

1. The various *Transactions and Concordats between Sovereigns and the See of Rome*;—a succinct and impartial history of them is wanting: the papal arrangements with Napoleon and Louis XVIII. would not be the least curious parts of such a work.

2. The *Councils of Basil, Pisa, Constance, and Trent.*

Separate histories have been written of the councils of Basil, Pisa, and Constance, by M. L'Enfant, a Lutheran minister: that of the council of Constance is best executed; it contains an account of a fact of importance to the English nation, but not generally mentioned by her historians,—that the French ambassadors contended, before the council of Constance, that Christendom was divided into the four great nations of Europe, Italy, Germany, France, and Spain: and that all the less nations, among which they reckoned England, were comprehended under one or other of them; but the English asserted, and their claim was allowed by the council, that the British Islands should be considered a fifth and co-ordinate nation, and entitled to an equal vote with the others.

In the different atmospheres of Venice and Rome, the history of the council of Trent has been written by the celebrated Fra Paolo, (the translation of whose work, with notes by Dr. Courayer, is more valued than the original), and by Cardinal Pallavicini. The Cardinal does not dissemble, that some of the deliberations of the council were attended with intrigues and passion, and that their effects were visible in various incidents of the council: but he contends, that there was an unanimity in all points which related to doctrine, or the reformation of manners: and Dr. Courayer, in the Preface to his translation, concedes, "that, in what regarded "discipline, several excellent regulations "were made according to the antient spirit "of the church;" and observes, "that though "all the disorders were not reformed by the "council, yet, if we set aside prejudice, we "may with truth acknowledge, they are in-"finitely less than they were before." The classical purity and severe simplicity of the style in which the decrees of the council are expressed, are universally admired, and are greatly superior to the language of any part of Justinian's law. In what concerns faith or morals, the decrees of the council of Trent have been received, without any restriction, by every Roman Catholic kingdom: all its decrees have been received by the Empire, Portugal, the Venetians, and the Duke of Savoy, without any *express* limitation; they have been received by the Spaniards,

Neapolitans, and Sicilians, with a caution, as to such points of discipline as might be derogatory to their respective sovereignties; but the council was never published in France. No attempt has ever been made to introduce it into England. Pope Pius the fourth, sent the acts of the council to Mary Queen of Scots, with a letter dated the thirteenth of June 1564, urging her to have the decrees of the council published in her dominions; but nothing appears to have been done in consequence of it. See *Histoire de la Reception du Conseil de Trente, dans les différens Etats Catholiques;* Paris, 2 vols. 8vo. 1766.

3. *The Bullarium*, or the collections which have been made of the Bulls of Popes;—the best of these collections is that printed at Luxemburgh or Geneva in 1771. It extends to the year 1753.

4. To these are to be added, *Regulæ Cancellariæ Romanæ*, or the Rules of the Roman Chancery, a court instituted by the see of Rome, for preparing and transmitting the receipts and letters of the pope; *the sentences and ordinances of the various congregations of cardinals at Rome; and the decisions of the*

Rota, the supreme tribunal of justice at Rome, both for its spiritual and its temporal concerns.

5. These complete the body of the Canon Law.—It should be observed, that, in addition to it, every nation in Christendom has its own national Canon Law, composed of *Legatine, Provincial, and other Ecclesiastical Constitutions*. The Legatine Constitutions of England are the ecclesiastical laws enacted in national synods, held under the cardinals Otho and Othobon, in the reign of Henry the Third. The Provincial Constitutions are principally the decrees of provincial synods, held under divers Archbishops of Canterbury, and adopted by the province of York, in the reign of Henry the Sixth. "At "the dawn of the Reformation," (Sir William Blackstone, Comm. 1 vol. Ints. sec. 3.), "in the reign of King Henry the Eighth, it "was enacted in parliament that a review "should be had of the Canon Law; and, till "such review should be made, all canons, "constitutions, ordinances and synodals pro-"vincial, being then already made, and not "repugnant to the law of the land, or the

"king's prerogative, should still be used and "executed. And, as no such review has "yet been perfected, upon this statute now "depends the authority of the Canon Law in "England.

"As for the canons enacted by the clergy "under James the First, in the year 1603, "and never confirmed in parliament, it has "been solemnly adjudged, upon the princi- "ples of law, and the constitution, that "where they are not merely declaratory of "the antient Canon Law, but are introduc- "tory of new regulations, they do not bind "the laity; whatever regard the clergy may "think proper to pay them."

VI.

With respect to the AUTHORITY OF THE CANON LAW, from which, in the present case, the part of it anterior to Gratian's decree, and subsequent to the Extravagantes Communes, must be excluded; it is composed of texts out of the Bible, passages from the writings of the fathers, the canons of general and particular councils, the decrees and rescripts of popes, and various other insertions and extracts. In each of these particulars, it possesses all the authority which the extract itself has; besides which, it possesses all the weight and authority, which it has acquired, by its having been so much adopted by courts, appealed to in disputes, taught in the schools, and praised and commented upon by the learned men of every state of Christendom. With more or less limitation, it forms the basis of the ecclesiastical law of every country, where the Roman Catholic religion is professed; and, speaking generally, in protestant countries, it has the force of law, when it is not repugnant to the law of the land.*

* The works, principally used in framing this account are, *Fleury's Institutions du Droit Ecclesiastique; his Discours sur l'Histoire Ecclesiastique; bishop Gibson's learned but very high-church Preface to his Codex Juris Ecclesiastici Anglicani*; *lord Hardwicke's argument in the case of Middleton v. Crofts, 2 Atk.* 650; *Pehem's Prælectiones in Jus Ecclesiasticum Universum, Lovanii,* 4 *vols.* 8*vo.* 1787; *Boehmer, Jus Ecclesiasticum Protestantium, Halæ Magdeburgicæ,* 6 *vols.* 4*to.* 1756; *Gerhard Von Mastricht Historia Juris Ecclesiastici et Pontificii, Duisburgii ad Rhenum,* 8*vo.* 1676; *Doujat's Histoire du Droit Canonique, Paris,* 8*vo.* 1677; *Van Espen's Jus Ecclesiasticum Universum, Lo-*

vanii, 6 vols. fol. 1753, a work, which, for depth and extent of research, clearness of method, and perspicuity of style, equals any work of jurisprudence which has issued from the press; but which, in some places, where the author's dreary Jansenism prevails, must be read with disgust:—a methodical and learned work with this title, "*Quis est Petrus? Seu Qualis Petri Primatus?* "*Liber Theologico-Canonico Catholicus. Editio* "*secunda, correctior et emendatior, cum Appro*-"*batione, Ratisbonæ* 1791;" the ablest work, in support of the papal prerogatives against the doctrines of the Sorbonne, which has come to the writer's knowledge. The account, given in it, of Isidore's Decretals is particularly interesting. *The Religionis Naturalis et Revelatæ Principia of Doctor Hook, Paris,* 3 *vols.* 8*vo.* 1774; the third volume of this work is, perhaps, the best treatise extant, on the ecclesiastical polity of the church, according to the notions of the Sorbonnists. It deserves to be more known in this country; it must have given the French divines an high opinion of the perspicuity and precision of English writing.

APPENDIX.

APPENDIX.

NOTE I.

THE ALPS begin with Col del Angentera, which lies to the west of a supposed line from Monaco to the Mons Visulus, or Monte Viso. Thence, they proceed, in a semicircular line of about 500 miles, first, on the south-eastern limits of France, afterwards on the southern limits of Swisserland, the Grisons, and the Tyrol, and then on the western limits of Styria, Carinthia and Carniola to the Sinus Flanaticus, or the Gulf of Cornero on the Hadriatic.

1. The *Alpes Maritimæ* take their name from the sea of Genoa, and extend from it up to Mons Visulus or Monte Viso. The most noted mountains in this part of the Alps are the Camellon and the Tendé.

2. The *Cottian Alps* reach from Monte Viso to Mount Cenis; they received their appellation from a territory of that name, of which Suza was the metropolis; they contain the Mons Matrona, or the Mont Genevre, whence the river Durance springs.

3. The *Alpes Graiæ* extend over Le Petit St. Bernard, the scene of the martyrdom of the Theban legion, to the Mons Jovis, or Le Grand St. Bernard. Hitherto the direction of the Alps is to the north.

4. On the northern side of that part of the Rhone, which flows over Valais into the lake of Geneva, are the *Alpes Helveticæ*; on its southern side are the *Alpes Penninæ*, the eastern chain of which is called *Alpes Le-*

pontinæ: they extend to the Mons Summus, or Mont St. Gothard.

5. The *Alpes Rhœticæ* extend from Mont St. Gothard over the Mons Adula, or the Adule, where the two fountains of the Rhine arise, to the source of the Drave. A mountainous country to the south of them, where the town of Trent lies, was called the *Alpes Tridentinæ.*

6. The *Alpes Noricæ* lie on the north of the Drave, and extend over parts of Austria, Styria, and Carinthia; not far from the close of them the *Alpes Pannonicæ* or Kahlemburgh mountains rise. The *Alpes Bastarnicæ* are the Carpathian mountains, the boundary of Hungary on the north and east.

7. The *Alpes Carnicæ* lie on the south of the Drave, and reach to Nauportus or Leyback, where the Alpine heights of Italy properly close. Two ranges of mountains proceed from them; the *Alpes Venetæ,* which extend into the Venetian possessions on the Terra Firma, and *Alpes Juliæ,* which are spread over the country from Forum Julii, or Friuli, to the eastern extremity of the Hadriatic.

Where the Alpes Carnicæ end, the *Mons Albius* begins: the *Alpes Bebianæ,* or the Welebitchian, or Murlakan mountains proceed from it, and extend southerly in a line of about 300 miles over Illyricum to *Mons Orbelus,* whence they branch into the Rhodope and Hæmus.

Such is the chain of the Alps: *the Appenines* are of equal celebrity. They rise in the Col della Tende; after stretching on the east of the supposed line from the Portus Monæci to Mons Vesulus, along the Gulf of Genoa, at no great distance from the coast, they proceed eastwardly to the centre of Italy, and afterwards to the south, always approaching nearer to the eastern than to the western coast. After they arrive at the Mons Gargamus, they take a south-westernly direction, and reach the Calabrian extremities of Italy. This account of the Alps is taken from *Cluverius's Ital. Ant. lib.* I. *ch.* 30, 31, 32; *Cellarius's Geog. Ant. lib.* 2; *Busching's Geography; Chauchard's Map, published by Stockdale; Bergier's Histoire des Grands Chemins de l'Empire Romain,* 2 *vols.* 4*to. Bruxelles* 1738; *and Mr. Pinkerton's Geography.*

NOTE II.

THE following account of the PRÆTOR'S JUDICIAL POWER, and its variations, is given by Doctor Bever, in his History of the Legal Polity of the Roman State, B. ii. c. 6.

" Originally, no more than one prætor was appointed; but, as the splendour and reputation of this illustrious city daily drew to it a vast conflux of strangers, the judicial business increased beyond the power of a single magistrate to dispatch. This demanded, therefore, the creation of a second, to preside over the causes of foreigners; from whence he was called " Prætor Peregrinus," to distinguish him from the former, who from the particular objects of his magistracy, was styled " Urbanus." When the empire received a further augmentation from the conquered provinces, each of these was allowed its provincial judge, with similar title and power.

Another century introduced a new refinement upon this institution. As the objects of judicature, both criminal, and civil, multiplied apace, and a great variety of new causes arose, very distinct, in their nature from each other, for the more easy and expeditious administration of justice, it was found necessary to throw them into distinct classes, called " Quæstiones," and to assign particular jurisdictions and judges to each, who were intituled Prætors and Quæsitors. These were obliged to exercise their respective jurisdictions within the city for the space of one year, after which they were dismissed into their several provinces, under the character of Pro-prætors. These great officers, of whatever rank or denomination, were first elected by the people, in the "comitia "centuriata;" but the right of assigning them to their particular provinces belonged to the senate.

The prætorian edicts, which constitute that branch of the old civil law now under consideration, were certain rules or forms, published by every prætor at the entrance upon his office, on the calends of January, signifying the methods whereby he proposed to administer justice during that year. These were hung up in the public court on a white table for the inspection of suitors and practitioners; but the authority of them lasted no longer than the office itself, unless they received a fresh ratification from the successor, and in that case they were called "Edicta "Translatitia."

The prætor had no power to abrogate or alter the laws, but only to temper them with equity, to apply them to the particular cases before him, according to his own ideas of justice, and to supply whatever was wanting to give them their full and proper effect. His edicts, therefore, were considered only as the voice of the law, but not law in its most comprehensive meaning, unless they happened to be adopted and continued by succeeding magistrates; under which qualified character only they are considered by Justinian himself. But notwithstanding their inferiority of rank in the scale of legislation, they were yet held in the highest esteem by some of the greatest princes and statesmen in after times, and by none more than himself, as appears from his inserting so large a number of them in the Digest.

In process of time, indeed, as the age grew more corrupt, and as these judges were more intent upon their own private views and emolument than upon a punctual and faithful administration of justice, they were very apt to vary even from their own edicts, when it happened to suit the convenience and interest of their friends or themselves. This opened a door to many shameful acts of injustice, and once more called forth that truly patriotic tribune, Caius Cornelius, under whose influence a law was enacted, to oblige the prætors to adhere to certain established rules, and not to depart from those which they themselves had laid down, at the entrance upon their respective magistracies."

NOTE III.

THE following account of THE MODES OF QUOTING THE CIVIL AND CANON LAWS is taken from *Dr. Hallifax's Analysis of the Roman Civil Law*, Camb. 1775, Note on page 2.

" It may not be amiss, for the sake of Beginners, to explain here the method of *quoting* the several parts, which now compose the CORPUS JURIS ROMANO-CIVILIS. The INSTITUTIONS are contained in Four Books: each Book is divided into Titles; and each Title into Paragraphs; of which the first, described by the Letters *pr.* or *princip.* is not numbered. The DIGESTS or PANDECTS are in Fifty Books: each Book is distributed into Titles; each Title into Laws; and, very frequently, Laws into Paragraphs, of which the first is not numbered. The CODE is comprized in Twelve Books; each of which is divided, like the Digests, into Titles and Laws; and, sometimes, Laws into Paragraphs. The NOVELS are distinguished by their Number, Chapter and Paragragh.

The old way of quoting was much more troublesome, by only mentioning the Number, or initial Words of the Paragraph or Law, without expressing the number either of Book or Title.

Thus § *si adversus* 12 *Inst. de Nuptiis,* means the 12th Paragraph of the Title in the Institutions *de Nuptiis,* which Paragraph begins with the Words *si adversus*; and which a modern Civilian would cite thus, I. 1. 10. 12. So *l.* 30 *D. de R. J.* signifies the 30th Law of the Title in the Digests *de Regulis Juris:* according to the modern way, thus, D. 50. 17. 30. Again, *l.* 5. § 3. *ff. de Jurejur.* means the 3d Paragragh of the 5th Law of the Title in the Digests *de Jurejurando:* better thus, D. 12. 2. 5. 3. And here note, that the Digests are sometimes referred to, as in the last instance, by a double *f;* and at other times by the Greek Π or π.

The method of quoting the ROMAN CANON LAW is as follows. The DECREE, as said above, consists of Three Parts; of which the first contains 101 Distinctions, each Distinction being sub-divided into Canons: thus 1 *dist. c.* 3. *Lex* (or 1 *d. Lex*) is the first Distinc tion, and 3d Canon, beginning with the word *Lex.* The second part of the Decree contains 36 Causes; each Cause comprehending several Questions, and each Question several Canons: thus 3. *qu.* 9. *c.* 2. *Caveant* is Cause the 3d, Question the 9th, and Canon the 2d, beginning with *Caveant.* The third part of the Decree contains 5 Distinctions, and is quoted as the first part, with the addition of the words *de Consecratione,* thus *de Consecr. dist.* 2 *can. Quia corpus* (or *can. Quia corpus* 35 *dist.* 2. *d. Consecr.)* means the 2d Distinction, and the 35th Canon, of the Treatise *de Consecratione,* which Canon begins with *Quia corpus.*

The DECRETALS are in Three Parts; of which the first contains Gregory's Decretals in 5 Books; each Book being divided into Titles, and each Title into Chapters: And these are cited by the name of the Title, and the number of the Chapter, with the addition of the word *Extra,* or the capital letter X: thus, *c.* 3. *Extra de Usuris;* is the 3d Chapter of the Title in Gregory's Decretals, which is inscribed *de Usuris;* which Title, by looking into the Index, is found to be the 19th of the 5th Book. Thus also, *c. cum contingat* 36 *X. de Offic. & Pot. Jud. Del.* is the 36th Chapter, beginning with *Cum contingat,* of the Title in Gregory's Decretals, which is inscribed *de Officio et Potestate Judicis Delegati;* and which, by consulting the Index, we find is the 29th Title of the 1st Book. The Sixth Decretal, and the Clementime Constitutions, each consisting of 5 Books, are quoted in the same manner as Gregory's Decretals; only, instead of *Extra* or *X.* there is subjoined *in sexto* or in 6. and *in Clementinis* or in *Clem.* according as either part is referred to: thus *c. Si gratiose* 5. *de Rescript. in* 6. is the 5th Chapter, beginning with *Si gratiose,* of the Title *de Rescriptis,* in the 6th Decretal; the Title so inscribed being the 3d of the 1st Book: And *Clem.* 1. *de Sent. et Re Judic.* (or *de Sent. et R. J. ut calumniis. in Clem.)* (or *c. ut calumniis,* 1. *de Sent. et R. J. in Clem.)* is the 1st Chapter of the Clementine Constitutions, under the title *de Sententiâ et Re Judicatâ;* which Chapter begins with *Ut calumniis,* and belongs to the xith Title of the 2d Book.

The Extravagants of John the 22d are contained in one Book, divided into 14 Titles: thus *Extravag. Ad Conditorem. Joh.* 22, *de V. S.* means the Chapter, beginning with *Ad Conditorem,* of the Extravagants of John 22d; Title, *de Verborum Significationibus.* Lastly, the Extravagants of later Popes are called *Communes;* being distributed into 5 Books, and these again into Titles and Chapters: thus *Extravag. Commun. c. Salvator. de Præbend.* is the Chapter, beginning with *Salvator,* among the *Extravagantes Communes;* Title, *de Præbendis.*

Printed by James & Luke G. Hansard & Sons,
near Lincoln's-Inn Fields, London.